I0038327

AGILE
ESSENTIALS

YOU ALWAYS WANTED TO KNOW

KALPESH ASHAR

VIBRANT
P U B L I S H E R S

Agile
Essentials

You Always Wanted To Know

Paperback ISBN 10: 1-63651-005-1
Paperback EAN 13: 978-1-63651-005-7

Ebook ISBN 10: 1-63651-006-X
Ebook ISBN EAN 13: 978-1-63651-006-4

Hardback ISBN 10: 1-63651-007-8
Hardback ISBN 13: 978-1-63651-007-1

Library of Congress Control Number: 2020945832

This publication is designed to provide accurate and authoritative information in regard to the subject matter covered. The Author has made every effort in the preparation of this book to ensure the accuracy of the information. However, information in this book is sold without warranty either expressed or implied. The Author or the Publisher will not be liable for any damages caused or alleged to be caused either directly or indirectly by this book.

Vibrant Publishers books are available at special quantity discount for sales promotions, or for use in corporate training programs. For more information please write to bulkorders@vibrantpublishers.com

Please email feedback / corrections (technical, grammatical or spelling) to spellerrors@vibrantpublishers.com

To access the complete catalogue of Vibrant Publishers, visit www.vibrantpublishers.com

SELF-LEARNING MANAGEMENT SERIES

TITLE	PAPERBACK* ISBN

ACCOUNTING, FINANCE & ECONOMICS

COST ACCOUNTING AND MANAGEMENT ESSENTIALS	9781636511030
FINANCIAL ACCOUNTING ESSENTIALS	9781636510972
FINANCIAL MANAGEMENT ESSENTIALS	9781636511009
MACROECONOMICS ESSENTIALS	9781636511818
MICROECONOMICS ESSENTIALS	9781636511153
PERSONAL FINANCE ESSENTIALS	9781636511849

ENTREPRENEURSHIP & STRATEGY

BUSINESS PLAN ESSENTIALS	9781636511214
BUSINESS STRATEGY ESSENTIALS	9781949395778
ENTREPRENEURSHIP ESSENTIALS	9781636511603

GENERAL MANAGEMENT

BUSINESS LAW ESSENTIALS	9781636511702
DECISION MAKING ESSENTIALS	9781636510026
LEADERSHIP ESSENTIALS	9781636510316
PRINCIPLES OF MANAGEMENT ESSENTIALS	9781636511542
TIME MANAGEMENT ESSENTIALS	9781636511665

*Also available in Hardback & Ebook formats

SELF-LEARNING MANAGEMENT SERIES

TITLE	PAPERBACK* ISBN

HUMAN RESOURCE MANAGEMENT

TITLE	PAPERBACK* ISBN
DIVERSITY IN THE WORKPLACE ESSENTIALS	9781636511122
HR ANALYTICS ESSENTIALS	9781636510347
HUMAN RESOURCE MANAGEMENT ESSENTIALS	9781949395839
ORGANIZATIONAL BEHAVIOR ESSENTIALS	9781636510378
ORGANIZATIONAL DEVELOPMENT ESSENTIALS	9781636511481

MARKETING & SALES MANAGEMENT

TITLE	PAPERBACK* ISBN
DIGITAL MARKETING ESSENTIALS	9781949395747
MARKETING MANAGEMENT ESSENTIALS	9781636511788
SALES MANAGEMENT ESSENTIALS	9781636510743
SERVICES MARKETING ESSENTIALS	9781636511733

OPERATIONS & PROJECT MANAGEMENT

TITLE	PAPERBACK* ISBN
AGILE ESSENTIALS	9781636510057
OPERATIONS & SUPPLY CHAIN MANAGEMENT ESSENTIALS	9781949395242
PROJECT MANAGEMENT ESSENTIALS	9781636510712
STAKEHOLDER ENGAGEMENT ESSENTIALS	9781636511511

*Also available in Hardback & Ebook formats

What experts say about this book!

Agile Essentials is an excellent introduction to Agile for the newcomer. It is also not only an excellent review for the experienced practitioner, as it may cover areas that you may not be as familiar with. In my case, it was interesting to read the discussion on Earned Value Management and Contracting in Agile (Chapter 5). Games such as "Remember the Future" and "Speedboat/Sailboat" (Chapter 3) are welcome additions to my toolkit.

Well written, it is a fast read if you are knowledgeable on Agile yet it provides a lot of information to learn from.

> **– Jose Solera, PMP, CSM, CSPO, CSP**
> **Agile practitioner since the 1990s**

Agile Essentials is an excellent book to learn the foundational elements of Agile project management. Agile Essentials effectively outlines the key concepts that all Agile project leader, Scrum Master or Product Owner must know and master to become an effective manager of Agile projects. Specifically, I like the in-depth overview of the agile requirements elicitation techniques which are critical to developing, prioritizing and grooming a customer-responsive scope for any effective project. Moreover, the discussion on agile execution is effective easy to understand for students new to Agile project management. I highly recommend this book as a foundation text for new students learning agile project management. I'm eager to add this book as required for my introductory Agile Project Management class.

> **– Tim Mills, MBA, MS, CPL, ITIL, SS-GB, CSM, PMP**
> **Lead Instructor, Agile Project Management**
> **Harvard Extension School**
> **Harvard University, Cambridge, MA USA**

About the Author

Kalpesh Ashar is a management consultant and corporate trainer holding an MBA (Dean's Award Winner) from SPJIMR, one of Asia's top business schools, and an Engineering degree with honors in Electronics. He has over 23 years of experience in large organizations and start-ups in Asia, USA, and Europe.

Kalpesh has worked in several project management roles, like Senior Project Manager, Delivery Manager, and Program Manager. He is passionate about writing on management subjects. His techno-business background gives him a unique position to write on management topics that are easy to understand for non-MBA graduates. His books are authored in a simple to understand manner without unnecessary use of management jargons.

Preface

The buzz word going on for a few years has been Agile. However, it is still a black box to many people. Although there are many great books on Agile, most of them focus on one or a few of the Agile methodologies and several practices within them. This book takes a different approach. It concentrates only on describing the commonly used Agile practices and how to implement them.

In today's enviornment, we see projects and operations that fails to deliver successful outcomes. Most of them attempt to use the Agile concepts, albeit without complete knowledge of its process or implementation. The results, in most cases, are failure.

Agile Essentials You Always Wanted To Know seeks to guide you in your quest to understand the how and why of Agile. The book starts by describing why Agile should be used and what are the situations where it is applicable. It then goes on to describe the most common Agile practices from various methodologies. Emphasis is given in the application aspect of the Agile practices.

This page is intentionally left blank

Table of Contents

5   Agile Tracking and Reporting   129

6   Agile Project Management   149

Glossary   165

This page is intentionally left blank

Introduction

This book does not attempt to cover every facet of the Agile system, such an attempt would exceed the scope of a beginner's text. The objective is to provide a basic holistic approach to creating workplaces that draw on the talents of those doing the work. By focusing on those talents, organizations can deliver extraordinary value to their customers and other stakeholders for whom the work is being done. To do this, we will concentrate on the commonly used elements of Agile and those applications that have been shown to produce value added outcomes.

To know about Agile, it is important that we first understand what it is, where it fits, and why it came into being. This is where the book begins. It describes the basic concepts of Agile and its methodologies.

We then dig deeper into the most popular Agile methodology – Scrum. We then see various useful practices that are applied at various stages of work, like planning, execution, and reporting. It ends with some soft skill aspects about Agile leadership and team characteristics. After reading this book, you would be able to answer the following questions about Agile:

- When do we need to use Agile?

- What are basic Agile principles that should be applied?

- How does Scrum work?

- Which are the main Agile practices and how and when to apply them?

- How do the softer aspects of leadership and team working change in Agile?

This page is intentionally left blank

Chapter **1**

Agile Overview

In this chapter we shall look at what is Agile and why it is needed. We shall also learn the pre-requisites to use Agile, its main characteristics, and the myths around it. Here we shall take a brief look at the various popular Agile methodologies.

Key learnings:

- The meaning of Agile

- Background of Agile

- Applicability of Agile

- The Agile Manifesto

- Agile characteristics and the myths around it

- The most popular Agile methodologies – Scrum, XP, Lean, and Kanban

Agile is a word that has gained immense popularity in the recent decade or so. It is quite likely that you have heard about it from your colleagues, friends, customers, or other professional acquaintances. It is also quite possible that you have been involved in Agile projects yourself. Whichever be the case, there is a general realization out there that Agile is the way to go for executing work on a lot of projects and operations in future.

Even though Agile as a term has been used by several people, its understanding might still be hazy in their minds. In this chapter we shall try to clarify what Agile is and what it is not, where it is needed, why it is needed, its basic characteristics, and methodologies.

1.1 What is Agile?

Agile is simply a concept that states how work should be done. This work can be a part of a project or regular operations. The concept of Agile has several different implementations, which are called methodologies. These methodologies can either be applied individually to work or together in combination. Most common Agile implementations are a combination of several Agile methodologies.

Agile is not recommended for all kind of work. There are two pre-requisites that need to be satisfied to get the real benefits of Agile. There pre-requisites are:

1. **Work has high uncertainty in scope** – Scope means the work that needs to be done on the project or operations. In several cases, scope is quite clear in the minds of the customer and other stakeholders. However, in most cases,

the customer only knows some part of the problem. Hence, the solution providers are asked to take up a few known requirements to start off and learn as they go. In such cases, scope is not clear in the beginning and it evolves as the work progresses. This is especially common on projects, as scope on projects is progressively elaborated – clarified as the work progresses.

2. **Work involves "knowledge workers"** – The term "knowledge workers" stands for highly skilled resources. Work that requires such resources is best positioned to apply Agile concepts, as one of the key characteristics of Agile is to give a lot of decision-making authority to the team. Hence, the team needs to have the required skills to take proper decisions.

1.2 Need for Agile

Work was happening in the past even without Agile. Then the question that comes to mind is – why do we need Agile? In order to understand the answer to this question, let's look at how work happened in the past and what were the major drawbacks of that approach.

The traditional approach to perform work was to gather and document all the requirements in the beginning, plan all of them at once, and then begin execution.

This is depicted in the diagram below.

Figure 1.1

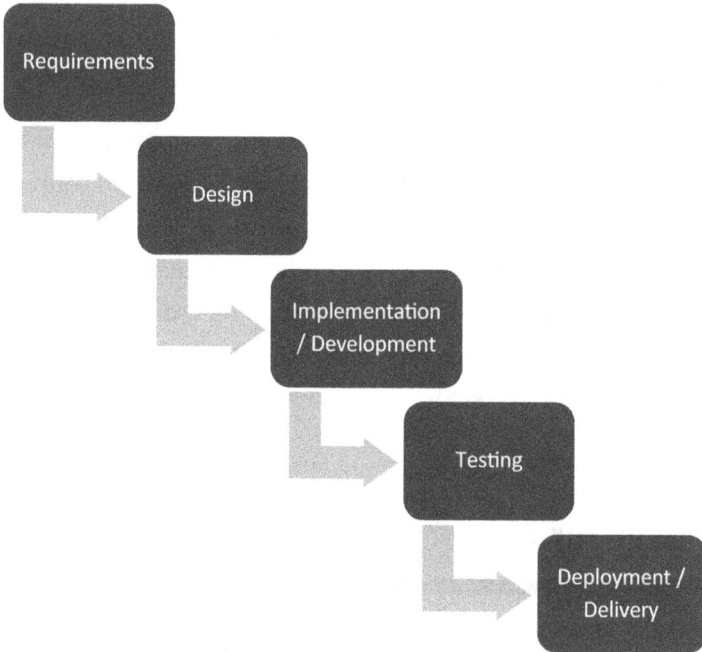

This kind of approach is termed as a "Waterfall Model" in software industry. However, similar model was being used in several industries, where each stage was done completely before moving to the next stage. When using this delivery approach, the customer gets to see the final deliverables only during later part of testing or during delivery stage. If at that time the customer does not like some of the deliverables and requests major changes, then one needs to go back to the previous stages of requirements, design, or development to incorporate them. This could involve a lot of rework, which involves time, effort, and money. Hence, making changes using this approach was quite cumbersome.

This approach is sometimes even referred to as the "Big Bang Approach", as all the deliverables are shown to the customer together at a later part of the project.

One other issue that arises with the above sequential approach is that if the customer needs to request for changes anywhere during the stages, for example, during development or testing, then once again that could involve a lot of rework by going back to the previous stages.

As we discuss above, handling changes could be quite a challenge in the sequential model. Due to this, the team is most often reluctant to incorporate changes in the work. This means that the team is not customer centric (does not concentrate on the customer's benefit). As appalling as this may sound, it is quite true.

This is where we enter the world of Agile. The main reason why Agile came into existence is in order to manage changes better. The term Agile comes from the term "Agility", which means our ability to change course rapidly and easily. Agile keeps customer benefit as the top priority by "embracing" changes. When we apply Agile, we always concentrate only on delivering what is beneficial to the customer.

The diagram below describes how work is done in Agile.

Figure 1.2

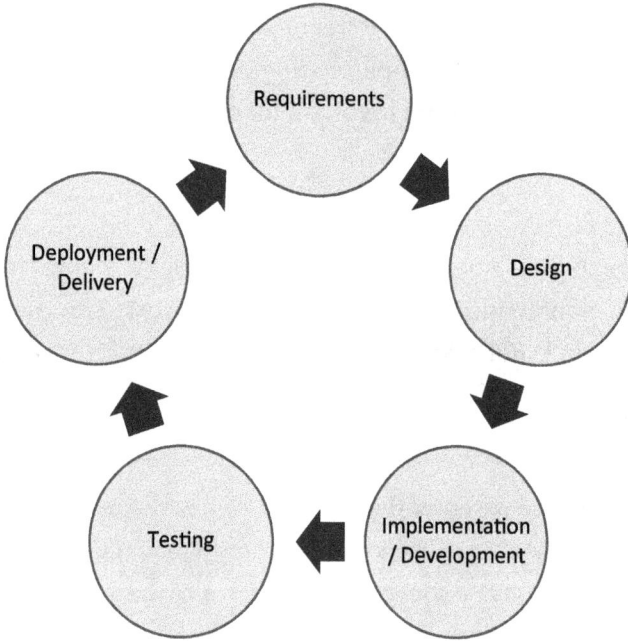

Work on Agile is done in short cycles called iterations, where each iteration consists of all the stages. The total work is completed by going through several such small cycles, each cycle delivering some part of the functionality.

1.3 Agile Characteristics

The key characteristics of Agile are as follows:

1. **Incremental** – The entire system is divided into pieces and
   built piece by piece. For example, if we have requirements
   for building various features of a system, and each feature
   is divided into sub-features, we will build all sub-features of
   one feature before moving to the next feature. This is shown
   in the diagram below:

Figure 1.3

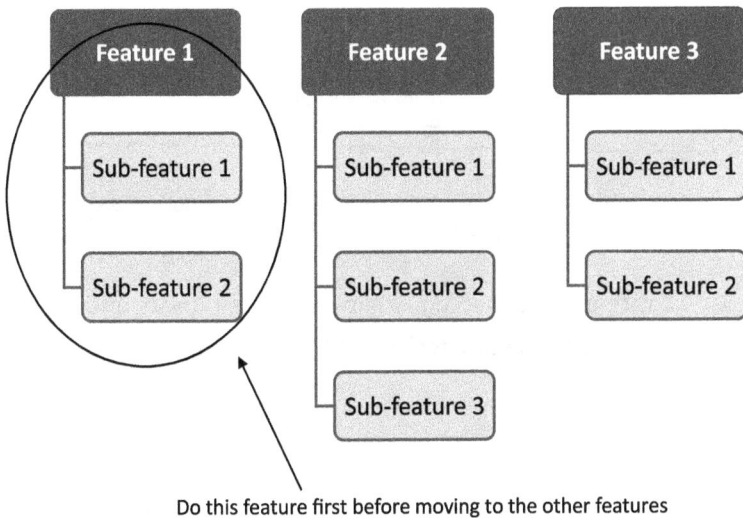

Do this feature first before moving to the other features

2. **Iterative** – A few initial parts of the system are built and
   improved upon as we get customer feedback. The entire
   system is built little by little and continuously improved
   until it is acceptable. For example, if we have requirements
   for building various features of a system, and each feature is

divided into sub-features, we will build a few sub-features of multiple features before moving to the rest of the sub-features. This is shown in the diagram below:

Figure 1.4

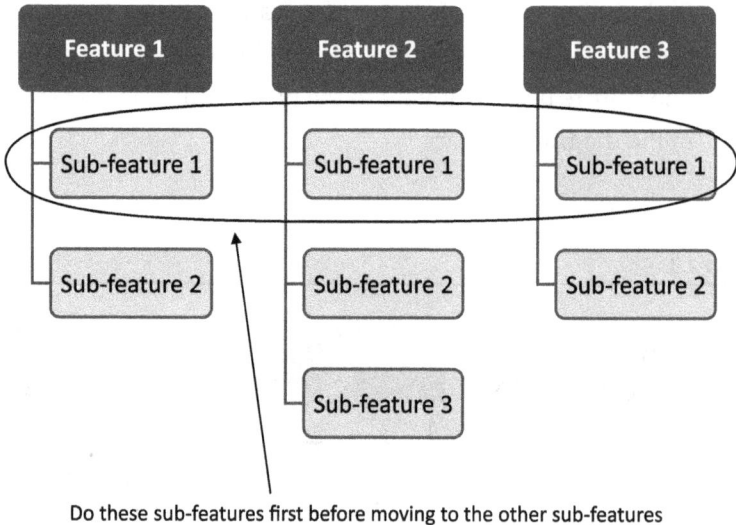

Do these sub-features first before moving to the other sub-features

3. **Adaptive** – Being able to change course rapidly and easily is one of the key characteristics and the foundation of Agile.

The main difference between traditional approach and Agile approach is as shown in the below diagram.

Figure 1.5

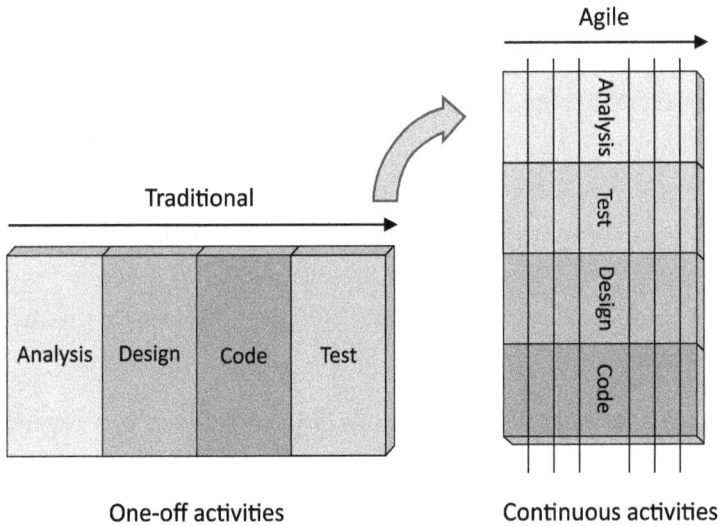

One-off activities   Continuous activities

Note: You may have noticed that Test is coming in an earlier stage in Agile. This is not a mistake but by design. We shall see later in this book a concept called Test Driven Development, that is commonly practiced in Agile.

1.4 Agile Myths

Over the years as Agile became popular, there have been several myths that have also crept in about it. Some of them could also be due to the human inertia to change. Here are these myths:

1. **It is a silver bullet that ensures success of a project** – It is seen that some people think that if their project is failing, they should introduce Agile and all the issues will get resolved and success will be guaranteed. This is not true. Agile does help in improving project success, but only when the pre-requisites (two pre-requisites described in an earlier section) are satisfied. However, it does not guarantee success.

2. **It does not require documentation** – Agile is about being customer centric by doing only value-added things and cutting waste. This means that critical documentation would still be made, but those documents that are less useful and seen as a waste, might not be made. So, making a statement that no documentation is needed is incorrect.

3. **There is no need to plan** – Planning in Agile is done in increments (parts) instead of all upfront planning. Planning might not be as detailed as in the traditional approach, but it does exist and done only to the extent that the team deems adequate.

4. **It does not need a disciplined approach** – There are several values, principles, and practices defined in various Agile methodologies that we follow. Some of them are stringent, but most of them are quite flexible and are left to the team to decide how and which ones to apply. This does not mean that it is not a disciplined approach; it is simply more

flexible in allowing selection and implementation of the approach.

5. **It involves a lot of rework** – This is exactly the opposite, as we get customer feedback for each iteration and build further. Due to this early feedback, the rework is in fact lesser than in the traditional approach.

1.5 Agile Manifesto

The work we do in Agile must adhere to the Agile Manifesto. This document was prepared by the founding fathers of Agile, and it consists of 4 values and 12 principles.

1.5.1 Agile Mindset

Figure 1.6

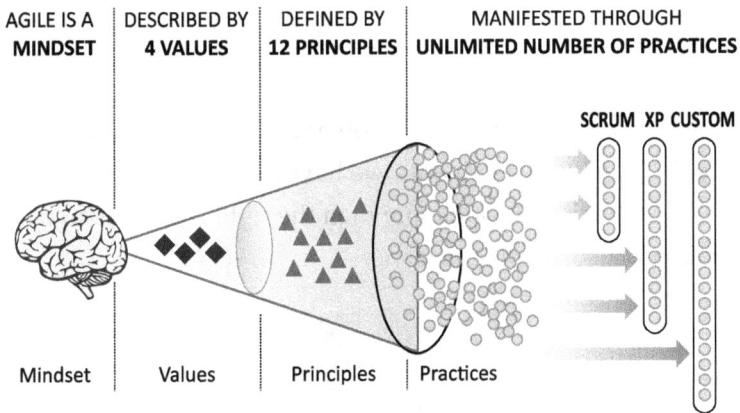

The Agile Mindset is the way we think in Agile. It starts with 4 values, that are further elaborated in 12 principles, which are finally converted to several practices. These practices are defined differently in the various Agile methodologies.

1.5.2 Agile Manifesto Values

Figure 1.7

The Agile Manifesto

Individuals And Interactions	over	Processes and Tools
Working Product	over	Comprehensive Documentation
Customer Collaboration	over	Contract Negotiation
Responding To Change	over	Following a Plan

That is, while there is value in the items on the right, we value the items on the left more.

www.agilemanifesto.org

The whole gambit of Agile revolves around the 4 Values seen above. In these four statements, we have a left side and a right side. We value the left side more than the right side, although the right side is also given importance.

Here is an explanation of each of these statements:

Individuals and interactions over Processes and tools

This means that in Agile we care more about individuals and their interactions than we care for following processes and tools. This does not mean that we do not have processes and tools, nor do we mean that we do not follow the processes. It means that although processes and tools do exist, they need to take a back seat when compared to people and communication. This statement states that our success depends more upon the kind of people we have and how effectively they can communicate with each other. It has lesser dependence on the processes and tools being used.

In traditional work environment more stress is put the process definitions and adherence. This leads to more predictable outcomes. However, on Agile, there is expected to be greater complexity and uncertainty. So, more importance is given to the people and communication to deliver the work successfully.

Working product over Comprehensive documentation

This statement states that we should concentrate on developing and delivering something of value, namely working product. Less focus should be put on developing detailed documentation as that adds lesser value to the customer. It does not mean that documentation is not important. However, a product that works is of greater importance.

In traditional way of doing work, we put a lot of focus on documentation as that reduces our dependency on individuals and makes it easier to maintain in future. However, several times the team loses focus on the actual deliverables while they make the accompanying documentation. Agile tries to fix this anomaly by providing higher priority to value adding deliverables. This, in no way means that documentation is not created. It simply means that we prioritize correctly so that we deliver greater value.

Customer collaboration over Contract negotiation

On Agile, we work closely with the customer and other stakeholders through daily collaboration. This may lead to constant change in work priority or scope. In such cases we try to accommodate the changes instead of going back to the contract and trying to negotiate with the customer. Hence, Agile contracts are also drafted in a different way so as to provide flexibility. This does not mean that we do not respect the contract terms, instead we give more importance to close collaboration with the customer and draft the contract accordingly.

Several times, we have rigid contracts with clear scope definition and any change has to go through a lengthy change control process. This makes it difficult to accommodate changes quickly. However, Agile work is expected to have greater uncertainty. Hence, we provide more flexibility in the contract so that the team can take on changes more easily. This is purely to ensure that the deliveries keep providing business value to the customer.

Responding to change over Following a plan

As discussed earlier, Agile came into existence so that changes can be managed better for greater business value. Hence, we try to accommodate changes, even late in development. It is more important to accept or embrace changes than to simply follow the original plan. In Agile, we do not do elaborate planning too far off as we know that changes could come up and we may need to make changes. Hence, we plan as we go. It does not in any way mean that Agile work does not have a plan. It means that Agile plans are more dynamic, and planning happens several times rather than just once during the early stage.

In the traditional way of working, we have planning stage that happens before execution starts. Most of the planning is done in that stage. However, on Agile there is greater uncertainty. Hence, we plan in chunks. This means that planning happens multiple times as changes are identified. This allows us to respond to changes better than following an original plan that is rigid and difficult to change.

1.5.3 Agile Manifesto Principles

Figure 1.8

01 Our highest priority is to satisfy the customer through early and continuous delivery of valuable software.

02 Welcome changing requirements, even late in development Agile processes harness change for the customer's competitive advantage.

03 Deliver working software frequently, from a couple of weeks to a couple of months, with a preference to the shorter timescale.

04 Business people and developers must work together daily throughout the project.

05 Build projects around motivated individuals. Give them the environment and support they need, and trust them to get the job done.

06 Agile processes promote sustainable development The sponsors, developers, and users should be able to maintain a constant pace indefinitely.

07 Working software is the primary measure of progress.

08 The most efficient and effective method of conveying information to and within a development team is face-to-face conversation.

09 Continuous attention to technical excellence and good design enhances agility.

10 Simplicity-the art of maximizing the amount of work not done-is essential.

11 The best architectures, requirements, and designs emerge from self-organizing teams.

12 At regular intervals, the team reflects on how to become more effective, then tunes and adjusts its behavior accordingly.

1. Our highest priority is to satisfy the customer through early and continuous delivery of valuable software.

This principle has 3 aspects. The first is about satisfying the customer through our deliveries. It means that we should always focus our work on what provides greater customer satisfaction. The second aspect is about early and continuous deliveries. It means that we try to prioritize requirements and deliver in chunks continuously throughout the lifecycle (incremental and iterative) with more value adding items early on. The final aspect is about delivering valuable software. It means that we should always strive to deliver something that adds value to the customer and not something that might be easy to build.

2. Welcome changing requirements, even late in development. Agile processes harness change for the customer's competitive advantage.

Changes in work are to add more customer value. Hence, we welcome them irrespective of when they are requested. We embrace changes to provide an edge to the customer.

3. Deliver working software frequently, from a couple of weeks to a couple of months, with a preference to the shorter timescale.

In Agile, we do not deliver everything in one go, say after 6 months. Instead, we make frequent small deliveries (incremental and iterative). This ensures that we keep adding value to the customer as we go and get early feedback from them. The suggested frequency for delivery is from two weeks to two months. This is referred to as an iteration in Agile. Typical iterations run for 2 weeks. Shorter iterations are preferred.

4. Business people and developers must work together daily throughout the project.

This principle is about collaboration in an Agile environment. It is important that business representatives and developers should be in daily contact so that queries can be answered faster, early feedback can be taken on deliveries, and changes can be understood better. In traditional projects, a lot of time is spent in getting answers from the customer or from the development team. In Agile, we promote daily communication, preferably face-to-face, so that quick responses can be received, and communication does not become a bottleneck.

5. Build projects around motivated individuals. Give them the environment and support they need, and trust them to get the job done.

People are our most important assets in work involving "Knowledge workers", where Agile is most used. Hence, this principle states that we should strive to have a motivated team and provide them with all they need and trust that they will deliver. The planning, decision making, and tracking are all left to the team to do as they are in the best position to do so as they understand the work better than anybody else. This contrasts with traditional management, where a manager performs these tasks.

6. Agile processes promote sustainable development. The sponsors, developers, and users should be able to maintain a constant pace indefinitely.

Agile work should appreciate the need for work-life balance of all stakeholders. The pace of the deliveries should be based on resource availability. Hence, we do not force delivery of certain scope on the team. Rather, we decide the scope to be delivered based on their availability. The pace that is set in early iterations should be sustainable (it is called velocity). This is possible when we base our deliveries on resource availability and not on overtime working as that leads to resource burnout and is not sustainable.

7. Working software is a primary measure of progress.

Measure of progress should be based on the value addition. And on software development work, value addition is directly proportional to working software delivered. Hence, the only way to measure the progress of our work is to track our delivery of working software and not on partially written, untested, or not-working software. When applied to non-software development work, this means that we measure progress on completed value adding deliverables rather than any other parameter.

8. The most efficient and effective method of conveying information to and within a development team is face-to-face conversation.

Face-to-face communication is the most preferred method of communication as it is the most effective. Hence, this principle promotes the use of this kind of communication as much as possible. This is true for both kinds of communication, within the development team, as well as with external stakeholders, like customer.

9. Continuous attention to technical excellence and good design enhances agility.

While we concentrate on delivering value to the customer, we should also ensure that we have given enough thought to making a good design and the development approach is technically

sound. If these are not thought of then we may have to redo a lot
of things later and that would slow down the pace of deliveries.

**10. Simplicity – the art of maximizing the amount of work not
done – is essential.**

On Agile, we focus on delivering the most valuable items
first and remove those items that do not add value. This is about
prioritizing requirements. We also try to build the valuable items
using a simple approach for early delivery and then build upon
them as we proceed rather than trying to deliver all at once. It is
best to concentrate on only a few most value adding items as they
provide most of the customer value. The other items provide little
value and are best left out. It is said that the 80/20 rule could be
applied to work that states that only 20% of the top items provide
80% of customer value.

**11. The best architectures, requirements, and designs emerge
from self-organizing teams.**

Agile teams are to be self-organizing. This means that there is
no formal organizational structure or a rigid hierarchy within an
Agile team. This helps in getting the right people take up work
that they can do best. They are also given decision making power
and ownership. This leads to better architectures, requirements,
and designs, and finally leads to better deliveries, greater value
addition, and higher customer satisfaction.

**12. At regular intervals, the team reflects on how to become more
effective, then tunes and adjusts its behavior accordingly.**

As we have seen, delivering customer value is one of the
most important aspect of Agile deliveries. Hence, the team needs
to keep a constant check on themselves on whether they are

delivering value. This is done by getting constant feedback from the customer and other stakeholders and doing fine tuning as per the recommendations. This is generally achieved on Agile using Retrospective session at the end of an iteration where we discuss learning from the just completed iteration. It is like Lessons Learned sessions on traditional work, but it is done much more frequently and not only at the end of all the work.

1.6 Agile Methodologies

Values and Principles of Agile are implemented through several Practices. These practices are defined as part of several Agile Methodologies. Many of these methodologies are not in much use these days. The list below gives a glimpse of most of the Agile methodologies:

- Scrum

- XP (eXtreme Programming)

- Lean (aligned closely to Agile, but not really an Agile methodology)

- Kanban (implementation of Lean)

- FDD (Feature Driven Development)

- Crystal

- DSDM (Dynamic Systems Development Method)

The most popular of the above is Scrum, followed by XP and Kanban. Very few practices of the other methodologies are used now.

In this chapter, we shall look at some of these methodologies in short. The next chapter is dedicated to Scrum.

1.6.1 Scrum

Figure 1.9

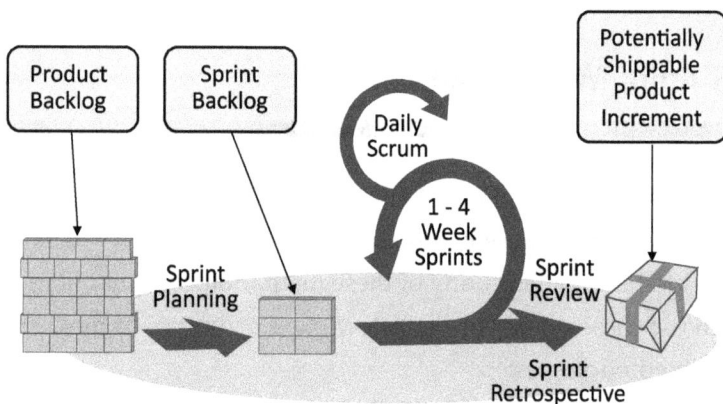

Scrum is based on short iterations called Sprints that generally go for 2 weeks. However, iteration length can be as short as 1 week or as long as a couple of months.

In Scrum, daily collaboration between all stakeholders happens through Scrum meetings or Scrum calls.

Retrospective meetings are held at the end of each iteration to incorporate continuous learning.

The next chapter is based entirely on Scrum, so more about this methodology later.

1.6.2 XP

Figure 1.10

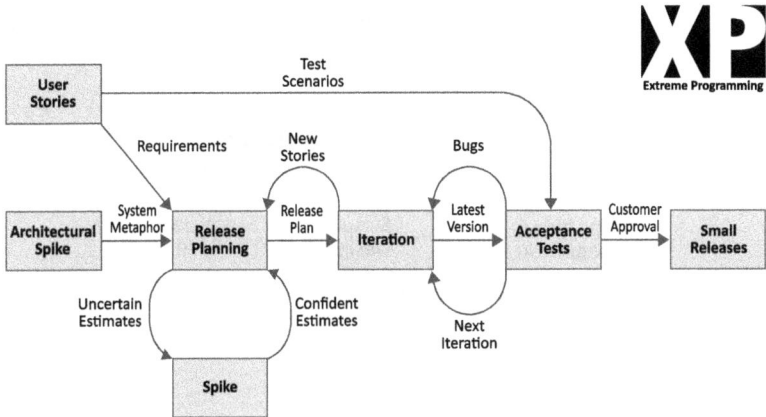

In XP, we start with user stories as requirements for the work. In case the technology to be used for the work is not yet proven then we may take up an Architectural spike to prove that the concept works. It is similar to proof of concept in traditional work.

Releases are planned by including user stories. A spike is work done in order to reduce risks. The word Spike is now widely used in general Agile practices to mean work undertaken in order to either reduce risks or to test a particular approach to see if it works.

Each release contains multiple iterations, which are tested using acceptance tests developed by the users. After approval, the iterations form part of small releases.

Figure 1.11

___

XP: Core Practices

Whole
Team

Collective Code
Ownership   Code
Standards

Customer   Test-driven
Tests   development

Refactoring   Planning
Games

Pair
Programming

Continuous   Simple   Sustainable
Integration   Design   Pace

Metaphor

Small
Releases

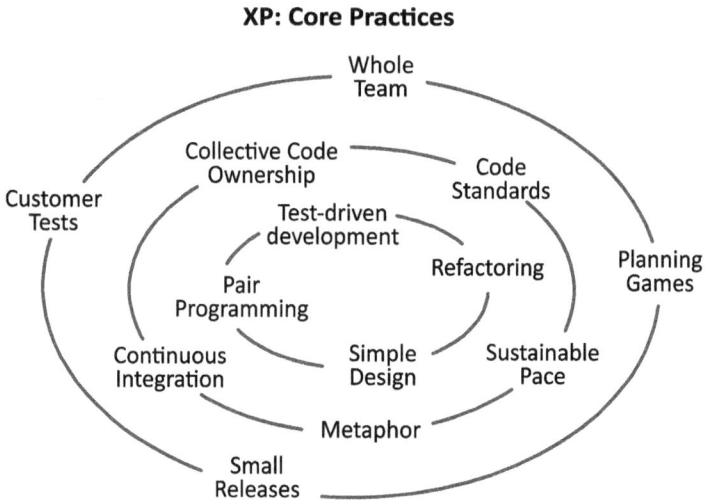

XP defines several core practices shown in the diagram above. Several of these are very commonly used in all Agile work. Below is a quick guide to these practices.

Whole Team

Whole Team refers to all contributors of the team working together towards success of the team. The customer provides requirements and anybody from the development team can take up the job of collecting requirements, creating design, coding, or testing. XP emphasizes on generalizing specialists and not role specialist. It means that nobody is fixed in a particular role for long and roles keep changing. This helps in efficient information sharing.

Planning Games

Planning Games refers to the games played during the planning activities performed on XP, namely release planning and iteration planning. These games can be for requirements elicitation, risk identification, estimation, prioritization etc. Several of these game are very popular.

Small Releases

Small Releases are encouraged in XP to demonstrate progress and to get early feedback from the customer. These releases are first put on the development environment and then onto other environments after thorough testing.

Customer Tests

Customer Tests practice refers to the fact that certain tests that refer to business scenarios are given by the customer and act as acceptance criteria for acceptance of deliverables. These tests are often automated by the team and executed to prove that the features are working.

Collective Code Ownership

Collective Code Ownership refers to the fact that nobody owns any particular piece of code. All the code is owned by the entire team and anybody is allowed to work on any piece of code.

Code Standards

Code Standards is about defining coding standards for the work, as collective code ownership could lead to inconsistencies in code. Hence, to avoid different approaches to coding, the entire team needs to follow consistent set of rules while coding.

Sustainable Pace

Sustainable Pace is about being able to deliver at the same pace throughout the life cycle. Putting extra hours and not being able to maintain work-life balance cannot be sustained for a long duration. Hence, these practices are to be avoided.

Metaphor

Metaphor refers to statements made to describe release or iteration features in a simple to understand way, so all stakeholders are able to know what is included in the release or iteration. For example, a statement like "The system will be able to take personal information from users" makes clear to all stakeholders that once delivered, the system will be able to perform this function.

Continuous Integration

Continuous Integration is a practice that states that every time new code is put in the code repository, it should be checked for compilation errors and some basic tests should be run to ensure that it does not break the already built functionality. This assists in finding problems early so they can be fixed earlier.

Test-Driven Development

Test-Driven Development states that the developer first develops the test cases for the user story to be developed. These test cases are run, and they would obviously fail as no code has been written for them to pass. Then the coding starts, and the objective of the developer is to get these test cases to pass. This

ensures that the developer focuses only on what is adequate to
get the test cases to pass and no extra code is written. This is a
commonly used practice in general Agile also and has been further
extended to include Acceptance Test-Driven Development where
even the User Acceptance Test Cases are developed and tested in
this way. We shall see it in detail in one of the later chapters.

Refactoring

Refactoring is about spending time to improve the design of
the already written code without changing the functionality. This
is so that the code remains maintainable and also speeds up future
development work. This practice is widely used in general Agile
now.

Simple Design

Simple Design means that we make a design that is the
simplest way to achieve what we want to develop right now. We
may iteratively build on it later on when new features are to be
built.

Pair Programming

Pair Programming practice encompasses the fact that two
programmers sit together when coding is done. One of them
writes the code, called Driver, and the other does real-time review
of the code being written, called Navigator. This ensures that
review is happening in parallel to coding. After a few hours, the
pair changes roles of Driver and Navigator. This practice also
helps in knowledge sharing.

Based on the above practices, an XP work's timeframe looks like the one shown in the diagram below.

Figure 1.12

Planning / Feedback Loops

Release Plan

Months

Iteration Plan

Weeks

Acceptance Test

Days

Stand Up Meeting

One day

Pair Negotiation

Hours

Unit Test

Minutes

Pair Programming

Seconds

Code

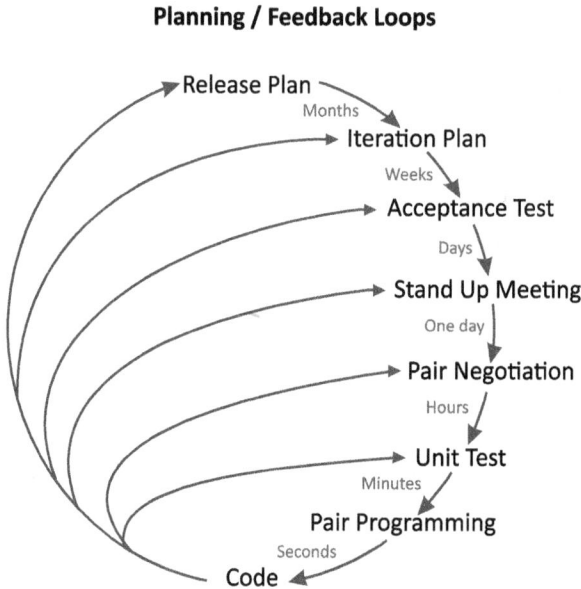

We start looking from the bottom of the figure where coding is done using pair programming on a real-time basis. The code that is written is unit tested as part of continuous integration within minutes and changes may be negotiated between the pair of programmers before finalization of the code.

In the daily stand-up meeting we get early feedback about work done and the customer runs acceptance tests at the end of the 2-week iteration to provide acceptance of deliverables. Iteration plans are created for each iteration and these roll up to the release that has a release plan.

1.6.3 Lean

The lean methodology comes from the field of manufacturing. It is based on Eliyahu Goldratt's Theory of Constraints (TOC). Strictly speaking, it is not an Agile methodology. However, the values of Lean are closely aligned to Agile practices – waste reduction and concentrating on delivering value.

Lean defines 7 core concepts:

Figure 1.13

Agile Lean Software Development

1. Eliminate waste

All wastes in the work should be removed to ensure that all our actions are adding value. For example, avoid partial work, reduce delays, avoid handoffs, and do not deliver any unnecessary features. This is similar to Agile principle of Simplicity, which says that we should concentrate our attention on delivering only value adding features and ignore others.

2. Empower the team

This is about avoiding micro-management and letting the team make local decisions. This concept is similar to Agile principle of Self-organizing teams.

3. Deliver fast

It means that we deliver value quickly in order to increase the return on investment of the customer.

4. Optimize the whole

This means that we should not look at improving the different pieces of the process separately. Any improvement or optimization should always be looked at from the end-to-end process point of view. For example, if we try to improve one part of the process, say testing, without analyzing which part of the process is contributing to the issues, we may not get the desired improvement in the output. Instead, we should study the process to find the bottleneck where improvement should be done and then improve those parts only.

5. Build quality in

This means that we should not concentrate only on testing after developing but also in-process. It means that we should ensure skilled resources are employed and they are made accountable for developing quality deliverables. Hence, we think of quality throughout the process and not just at the end after developing the product. This produces higher quality deliverables. Practices in Agile that align with this concept are refactoring, continuous integration, and unit testing.

6. Defer decisions

This is about maintaining a balance between early planning through early decisions and committing to things as late as possible. Delaying decision to the last responsible moment provides us with greater flexibility and decisions are taken when we have greater knowledge and hence lower risk.

7. Amplify learnings

This talks about getting early feedback on our deliverables from stakeholders and applying it on the process as improvement.

1.6.4 Kanban

Kanban is based on "lean" production system used at Toyota. Kanban in Japanese means "billboard" or "signboard". A Kanban system concentrates on the process's value stream. It is an implementation of a lean system.

There are 5 principles that govern a Kanban system.

Figure 1.14

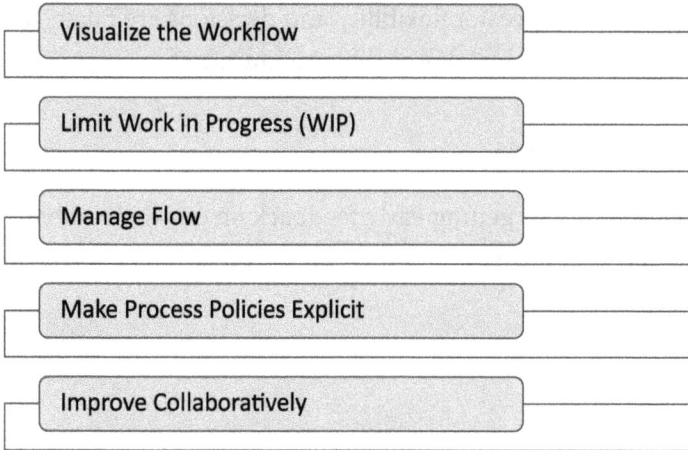

Visualize the Workflow

Limit Work in Progress (WIP)

Manage Flow

Make Process Policies Explicit

Improve Collaboratively

1. Visualize the workflow

Visualize the workflow means that we should articulate the process clearly to see how work flows through it. This helps in organizing, optimizing, and tracking it.

2. Limit Work in Progress (WIP)

Limit WIP is about setting a low work in progress limit at each stage of the process. It helps in identification of issues in the system and creates a pull system of work. It is done using Kanban or Task board that we will see later on in the book.

3. Manage flow

Manage flow is to track how work flows through the system to identify issues and fix them.

4. Make process policies explicit

Make process policies explicit is to make the entire team well aware of how things work so as to allow no ambiguities.

5. Improve collaboratively

Improve collaboratively is about using scientific measurements so the team can work collectively to make process improvements.

The key tool provided by Kanban is a Kanban Board / Task Board, which is almost universally used in all Agile work. An example board is shown below.

Figure 1.15

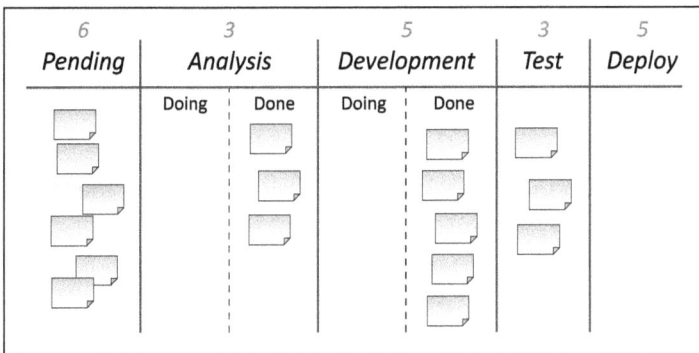

6	3		5		3	5
Pending	Analysis		Development		Test	Deploy
	Doing	Done	Doing	Done		

Each sticky note consists of a requirement, generally in the form of a user story. These notes are placed in the various columns to show where each of the work items are in the entire process.

WIP (Work in Progress) limits are put at each stage, written on the top of the stage. For example, we cannot have more than 5 requirements in Development stage at any time and no more than 3 can be in Analysis.

This shows a typical Kanban pull system where work is pulled from the previous stage only once work moves through the system. For example, once an item moves from Development to Test, only then an item can be pulled from Analysis into Development. This ensures that work does not get piled up at any stage leading to optimizing the whole rather than any particular stage.

WIP limits ensure that there is not too much multi-tasking, as that leads to task switching – a waste. In order to reduce this waste, WIP limits are put at each stage to ensure that too much work does not get piled up at any stage. The WIP limits are decided based on the team size and require a trial-and-error method. As a thumb rule, one can start with either 1 or 2 tasks per team member at any point of time while deciding the WIP limits, and then fine tune based on learnings – improve collaboratively. If there is too much idle time for any team member, then the WIP limit needs to be increased for that stage, and if there is a bottleneck team member identified at any stage, then the WIP limit needs to be reduced for that stage.

Chapter Summary

◆ Agile helps remove some of the drawbacks of the traditional approach of delivering – difficulty in managing changes and lack of customer-centricity. There are two pre-requisites to apply Agile – lack of scope clarity and "knowledge worker" team. Agile is both incremental and iterative.

◆ Agile Manifesto consists of 4 Values and 12 Principles. Each Agile Methodology defines its own Practices based on these. In the 4 Values, we give more importance to the item on the left than to the item on the right.

◆ Scrum is the most popular Agile Methodology. It consists of iterations called Sprints.

◆ XP is a software development centric Agile Methodology that provides 13 practices, many of which are quite popular.

◆ Kanban is a "lean" implementation that rests on 5 practices and in based on waste reduction. A Kanban Board is very commonly used in Agile.

Solved Examples

1. Which of these is NOT in the Agile Manifesto?

   a. Customer collaboration over contract negotiation

   b. Responding to change over following a plan

   c. Individuals and interactions over processes and tools

   d. Working product over partial delivery

Solution:

d. Working product over comprehensive documentation (sometimes also written as Working software over comprehensive documentation).

2. Which of these is not purpose of a Retrospective?

a. To figure out what was done well so team can be appreciated

b. To figure out what mistakes were made

c. To figure out process improvements

d. To figure out what changes should be made to the next sprint

Solution:

a. If retrospectives are linked with the team's appreciation, promotion, or hikes, then the team could become defensive and the purpose of the session to make improvements gets defeated.

3. Which one of these is NOT a waste?

a. Continuous improvement

b. Developing extra features

c. Delay introduced due to an unnecessary step

d. Partially completed work

Solution:

a. Continuous improvement. Making improvements are required in Agile and are not considered as a waste.

4. What are the main reasons for working in an Agile environment?

Solution:

   i. Better responsiveness to changes

  ii. Greater focus on providing value to the customer

5. Which Agile methodology gives the best results?

Solution:

The various Agile methodologies define different practices based on the Agile Manifesto. No single methodology is a fit-for-all. The most common way to implement Agile is by combining practices from various methodologies together to perform the work. Having said this, most development projects use Scrum as the pre-dominant methodology, with some practices of XP and Kanban. When working in an operations environment, the most pre-dominant methodology used is Kanban, with some practices of Scrum and XP.

Practice Exercises

1. What is the correct meaning of the Agile principle –
   "The most efficient and effective method of conveying
   information to and within a development team is face-to-face
   conversation"

   a. Agile teams should always be co-located

   b. Wherever possible, stakeholders should meet face-to-face

   c. Wherever possible, project team should meet face-to-face

   d. Written documentation should be little in Agile

2. Roles in pair programming are changed -

   a. Often

   b. At iteration finish

   c. Per release

   d. Not often

3. **A Kanban board contains -**

    a. Road signs

    b. Project instructions

    c. WIP limits

    d. Project plan

Solutions to the above questions can be downloaded from
the **Online Resources** *section of this book on*
www.vibrantpublishers.com

Chapter **2**

Scrum

T his chapter is dedicated to the Scrum methodology. Here we shall see the end-to-end architecture of Scrum. It also describes the various Scrum roles, the various Scrum events, and the various artifacts used or created in Scrum.

Key learnings:

- End-to-end view of Scrum methodology

- The roles in Scrum and their job description

- The events defined in Scrum and their purpose

- The different artifacts in Scrum

- A chronology of events in Scrum

As discussed in the last chapter, Scrum is the most popular Agile methodology. Let us look at the various key parts of Scrum.

2.1 Scrum Overview

Here is the overall architecture of the Scrum methodology.

Figure 2.1

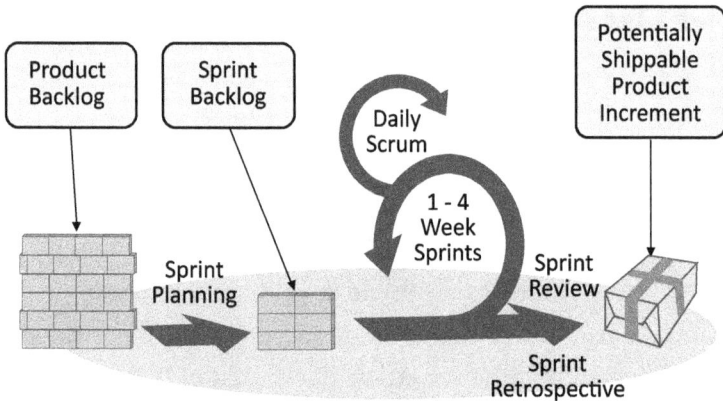

Let us start from the left of the diagram. The requirements are identified and put in a prioritized list called Product Backlog. Product Backlog consists of are all of the requirements, known now and the new ones that will be identified later on. All current and new requirements are included in the same Product Backlog. Hence, it is a one-stop shop for requirements on Scrum.

The work is planned to be done in various iterations called Sprints. A Sprint Planning meeting is held to select some of the items from the Product Backlog. These are put in the Sprint Backlog.

A Sprint generally lasts 1-4 weeks and the objective is to deliver all items from the Sprint Backlog. A daily Scrum meeting is held in order to track progress. A Sprint is time boxed. This means that its duration cannot change irrespective of whether all the items have been successfully delivered or not. Undelivered items are moved back to the Product Backlog to be taken up in a future Sprint. Duration of Sprint never changes. No matter what.

At the end of the Sprint, a Sprint Review is held to check completion of items and signoffs, followed by a Sprint Retrospective to discuss learnings from the Sprint.

Each Sprint is expected to deliver a potentially shippable product increment.

2.2 Scrum Pillars

There are 3 pillars in Scrum as shown below.

Figure 2.2

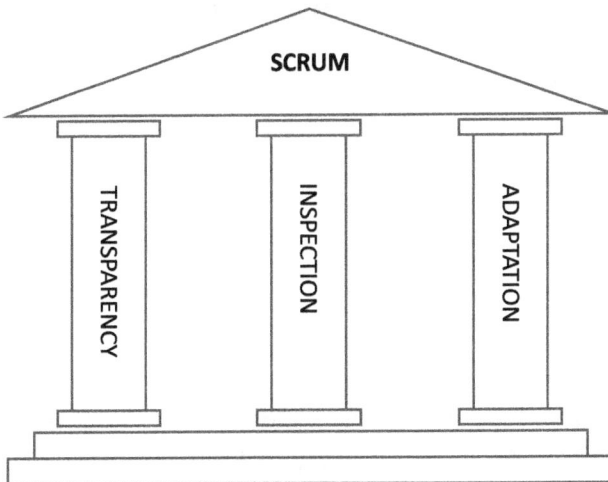

Scrum rests on 3 pillars – Transparency or Visibility, Inspection, and Adaptation.

Transparency – Transparency means that all stakeholders have a visibility to what is being done and where we stand. It also encompasses the fact that all parties are involved in deciding what will be the acceptance criteria for each deliverable. This is referred to as the definition of "Done".

Inspection – Inspection is done in Agile on a continuous basis to check the work progress towards achieving its goals and correcting any deviations early on. This is done daily using the Scrum meetings.

Adaptation – Adaptation is somewhat related to inspection to ensure that any deviations are taken care of to avoid failure.

2.3 Scrum Roles

There are 3 roles defined in Scrum.

2.3.1 Product Owner

Product Owner represents the customer and is responsible and accountable for the requirements, managing the product backlog, prioritizing items in the backlog, accepting deliverables, and providing support required by the development team from the business front. Product Owner is solely responsible to maximize value of the product being delivered. He also creates a product vision and shares it with all other members of the scrum team.

2.3.2 ScrumMaster

ScrumMaster is a servant leader who is responsible for removing impediments to progress and facilitating various scrum events. He also acts as a bridge between product owner and development team for communicating vision, goals, and backlog items. The term "servant leader" means that the ScrumMaster does not manage the team. He rather performs administrative tasks for them to ensure that they concentrate on delivering items from the backlog. ScrumMaster should not be mapped to a traditional Project Manager role as the latter manages the project whereas the prior facilitates things on the project for the self-organizing development team.

2.3.3 Development Team

Development Team consists of resources with skills that are adequate to deliver all the work. It is a self-organizing cross-functional team. It is recommended to keep this team small, ranging from 5 to 9 people. It is also recommended that the development team should not change during the Sprint but may change across Sprints.

All the three roles - Product Owner, ScrumMaster, and Development Team, put together is referred to as the Scrum Team.

Apart from the Scrum Team, there could be other stakeholders, like Project Manager, Organization, Users etc. These roles are not specifically defined in Scrum, but they may exist.

It should be noted that the 3 roles defined in Scrum are committed to the work. Whereas the other stakeholders whose roles are not defined in Scrum may be involved in the work. Committed roles are often termed as Pig in breakfast and involved roles are termed as Chicken in breakfast. This is because pig gives itself completely in breakfast as bacon, but chicken only contributes eggs for breakfast.

2.4 Scrum Events

Several events are used in Scrum, however not all of them are defined as part of the Scrum methodology. They are described below.

1. Strategy Meeting (often used but not defined in Scrum)

Strategy Meeting is a kickoff meeting held to discuss product strategy, to come up with a product vision, define epic user stories (high-level requirements), define detailed user stories, to make product backlog, and to create product roadmap.

Epic user stories are requirements at a high-level. Requirements on Agile are generally in the form of user stories that we shall discuss in a later chapter. Product backlog contains all items that need to be delivered for the product and product roadmap is a pictorial view of the requirements included in each release. Work is broken down into releases which are further broken down into iterations. A Strategy Meeting should happen at least once in 12 months and the duration is generally 4-16 hours. All the stakeholders are invited to this meeting.

2. Release Planning Meeting (often used but not defined in Scrum)

Release Planning Meeting is held for each release to decide prioritization of requirements in the product backlog, decide what should be included in the release, and put high-level estimates against each item in the product backlog. Product Owner is in-charge of this meeting and all stakeholders are invited to attend it. It generally runs for 4-8 hours.

3. Sprints (defined in Scrum)

Sprints are time boxed iterations of 1 to 4 weeks, most often done for 2 weeks. They build a potentially releasable product increment. Several Sprints make up a Release and several Releases make up a Project.

4. Sprint Planning Meeting (defined in Scrum)

Sprint Planning Meetings are held by the Product Owner to do detailed estimation of stories in the product backlog and agree on which ones can be taken up in the sprint and put in the sprint backlog. The decision on which stories to include depends upon the priority set by the Product Owner and the risks perceived by the Development team. We try to deliver those stories that provide the most business value first. Sprint Planning meeting generally includes only the Scrum Team consisting of Product Owner, ScrumMaster, and Development Team. Its duration is about less than 2 hours per week of length of the Sprint. For example, if the Sprint is for 2 weeks then this meeting goes for about 4 hours.

5. Daily Scrum Meeting (defined in Scrum)

Daily Scrum is a meeting that is organized on a daily basis and is time boxed to a maximum of 15 minutes. Irrespective of anything, the duration should never cross 15 minutes.

Invitees generally include the Development Team, Product Owner, and ScrumMaster. Only the Development Team is allowed to speak. They only provide an answer to three questions:

1. What has been achieved yesterday

2. What will be achieved today

3. What are the obstacles in the work

No other points are allowed to be discussed. This is ensured by the ScrumMaster. Any other issues or risks are put in a "Parking lot" to be taken up later offline with only the required stakeholders.

6. Sprint Review Meeting (defined in Scrum)

Sprint Review Meeting is held at the end of the Sprint to present what work has been completed. Development Team shows the "Done" items to the Product Owner and other stakeholders. This is about getting acceptance of work done, also referred to as Scope Validation in traditional project management. Future plans for next Sprint may also be discussed in this meeting that runs from 1-2 hours.

7. Sprint Retrospective Meeting (defined in Scrum)

Sprint Retrospective Meeting is the last event to be held after Sprint Review. In that meeting we invite only the Scrum Team to discuss what went right and what went wrong during the just completed Sprint. This learning is documented so we can improve our processes or the way of working in later Sprints. It goes for 1-3 hours. As a thumb rule it goes for 45 minutes per week of length of Sprint. For example, if the Sprint was for 2 weeks then this meeting goes for about 1.5 hours.

8. Product Demo (often used but not defined in Scrum)

A Product Demo may be done at the end of a release to showcase the achievements in the release. The development team shows the new product features that were developed during the release.

2.5 Scrum Artifacts

Various artifacts are created in Scrum. All of these are seen as adding value to the customer, hence they are all needed. Apart from these, the team may decide if any other artifacts are needed, and if so, make them. However, we should always uphold the thinking of only making those artifacts that are deemed necessary to add value to the customer.

Below are the various artifacts, some of which are defined in Scrum and others are not defined in Scrum, but commonly used.

1. Product Vision (often used but not defined in Scrum)

Figure 2.3

> **To build a software application that will assist in buying and selling of bikes**

A Product Vision Statement is a statement that is created during the Strategy Meeting that describes the business vision. It gives a view to all involved about why the work is being undertaken and what to expect from it.

2. Product Roadmap (often used but not defined in Scrum)

Figure 2.4

Product Roadmap

2013	2014	2015
• Feature	• Feature	• Feature
• Feature	• Feature	• Feature
• Feature	• Feature	• Feature
• Feature	• Feature	• Feature
• Feature	• Feature	• Feature
• Feature	• Feature	• Feature

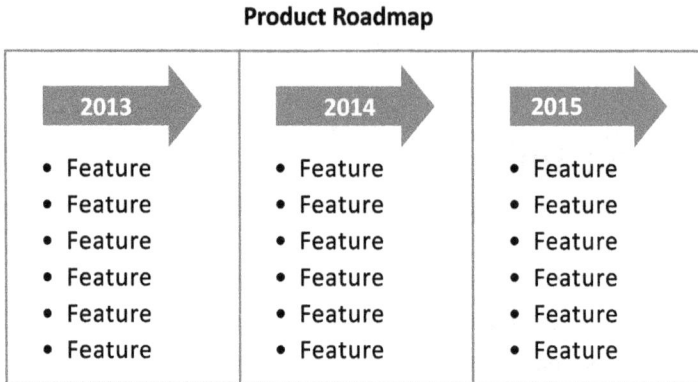

Product Roadmap is a pictorial representation of which features would be delivered in which release. We shall look at this in more detail in one of the later chapters. It is also created during the Strategy Meeting.

3. Product Backlog (defined in Scrum)

Figure 2.5

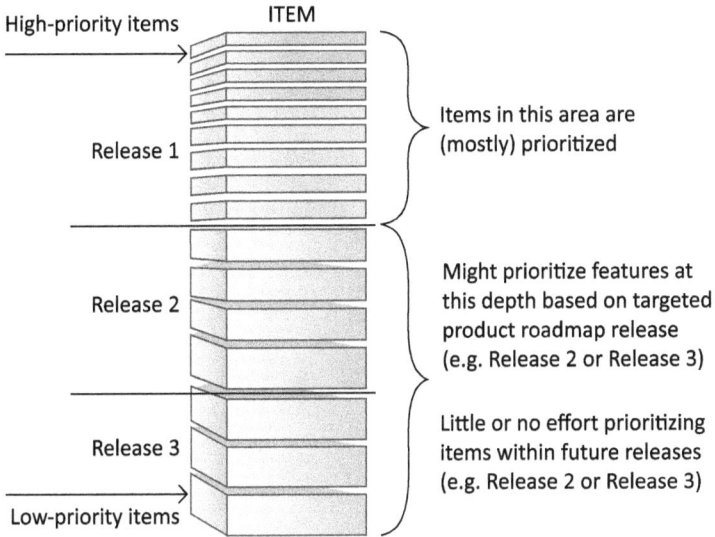

Product Backlog contains a list of requirements generally in the form of user stories. It is also created during the Strategy Meeting. It is arranged using priority from Product Owner based on which ones add how much business value. The prioritization process may also involve inputs on risks involved with the user stories. A Product Backlog may be changed to add more details, or to refine estimates. This is referred to as "Grooming" or "Refinement" of the backlog.

4. Release Backlog (often used but not defined in Scrum)

Release Backlog is created during the Release Planning Meeting and includes only those user stories that are to be delivered in that release. It is a subset of the Product Backlog.

5. Sprint Backlog (defined in Scrum)

Sprint Backlog is a subset of Release Backlog and contains only those user stories that are targeted to be delivered in the particular Sprint. It is also accompanied by a plan for the Sprint. It is created during Sprint Planning Meeting.

6. Definition of "Done" – DoD (defined in Scrum)

Definition of "Done" consists of completion actions required for deliverables in a sprint. For example, peer review, unit testing, and meeting acceptance criteria can be a part of this. Deliverables cannot be said to be completed until these actions have been successfully completed.

2.6 Scrum Chronology of Events

The diagram below gives the end-to-end chronology of events that take place when using Scrum.

Figure 2.6

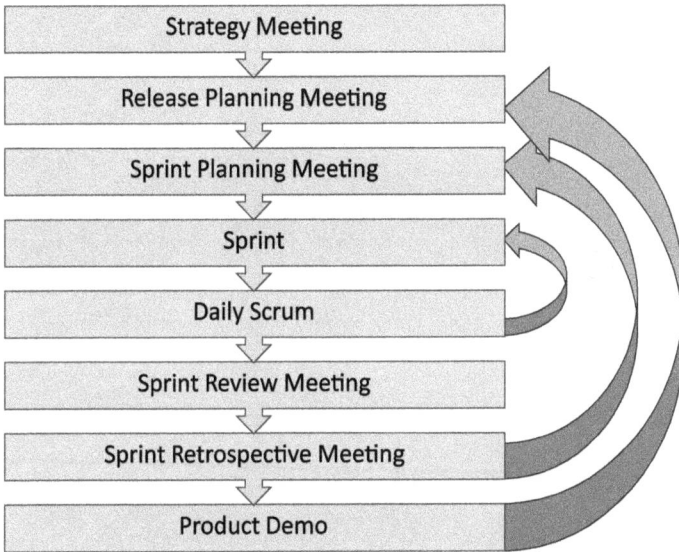

First the Strategy Meeting is held to make a Product Backlog. The work is then broken down into Releases, starting with the Release Planning Meeting and ending with the Product Demo.

Within a Release there are several Sprints that start with the Sprint Planning Meeting and end with the Sprint Review and Sprint Retrospective Meeting.

Within a Sprint, we have Daily Scrum Meeting or Call.

It may be noted that Releases are not specifically defined in Scrum. Only Sprints are defined. However, it is a common Agile practice that is used on Scrum to break the work into Release and then into Sprints.

Chapter Summary

◆ Scrum Methodology is the most popular Agile Methodology that has 1-4 weeks of iterations called Sprint.

◆ Scrum starts with a Product Backlog, from which a Sprint Backlog is created during the Sprint Planning Meeting based on prioritization done by the Product Owner. A Daily Scrum Meeting is held for a quick knowledge sharing of work done, going to be done, and any impediments. Sprint Review is held to showcase "Done" deliverables and Sprint Retrospective is for identifying improvements for the next Sprint.

◆ Strategy Meeting, Release Planning Meeting, and Product Demo may also be held, but are not defined in Scrum.

◆ Product Owner represents the business, ScrumMaster is the servant leader, and Development Team is a cross-functional implementation team.

◆ Product Backlog contains all requirements. Sprint Backlog contains only those requirements that the team would deliver in the Sprint. Definition of "Done" consists of criteria that need to be satisfied to say that a certain work is complete.

◆ Product Vision, Product Roadmap, and Release Backlog may also be created, but are not defined in Scrum.

Solved Examples

1. **A developer has an important point on the Daily Scrum. What should the ScrumMaster do?**

   a. Allow a detailed discussion as it is important to the project

   b. Ask the developer to send the point in writing to everybody to avoid any confusion

   c. Initiate a call later to discuss the point

   d. Add this point as a point of discussion during the project retrospective

Solution:

c. Initiate a call later to discuss the point – no detailed discussions happen on the daily scrum meeting. These are then taken up offline.

2. Sprint Review is held in order to -

a. Decide what to develop during the Sprint

b. Showcase completed product deliverables to the stakeholders

c. Estimate the time taken to develop the product deliverables

d. Discuss what went right and what went wrong during the Sprint

Solution:

b. Showcase completed product deliverables to the stakeholders – Sprint Review meeting is held at the end of each Sprint with the purpose of getting acceptances of "Done" deliverables.

3. What are the main benefits of using the Scrum methodology?

Solution:

i. Scrum is incremental and iterative, allowing for delivery in parts

ii. Sprints allow for early feedback from the customer

iii. Changes are easy to incorporate, as the team works on Sprint Backlog, not on the Product Backlog

iv. Team gets an opportunity to learn and make improvements at the end of each Sprint

Practice Exercises

1. **Which of these is NOT a Scrum concept?**

   a. Sprint Review

   b. Daily Scrum

   c. Sprint Retrospective

   d. Strategy Planning

2. **Out of the following which one contains the Sprint scope?**

   a. Sprint backlog

   b. Product backlog

   c. User stories

   d. Daily scrum

Solutions to the above questions can be downloaded from
the **Online Resources** *section of this book on*
www.vibrantpublishers.com

Chapter 3

Agile Planning

In this chapter, Agile planning techniques are discussed. We will look at how the team decides which features to include in the product. The chapter also describes the entire sequence of activities in planning - requirements gathering, prioritization, and estimation.

Key learnings:

- Understanding of MVP and MMP for a product

- Requirements gathering techniques

- Requirements prioritization techniques

- Techniques to estimate (do sizing) of requirements

Planning in Agile is not done all at once in the beginning. Instead, it is done several times throughout the lifecycle. This ensures that we can be more responsive to changes.

3.1 Agile Planning vs. Traditional Planning

Here are some of the main differences between planning in Agile and planning in the Traditional approach.

Figure 3.1

Traditional Plans	Agile Plans
• Created upfront at the start	• Only high-level plan created upfront with detailed planning only for the user stories in the next release or iteration
• Re-planning is lesser, only when changes happen	• Re-planning is the norm as we embrace changes
• Most requirements are known upfront	• True requirements are uncovered as we proceed
• Planning is mostly at the beginning of the lifecycle	• Planning is in lumps throughout the lifecycle
• Midcourse adjustments are few	• Midcourse adjustments are a norm

Traditional Plans are created upfront at the start of the lifecycle during the Planning stage. Agile Plans are created only at a high-level upfront with detailed planning only for the user stories in the next release or iteration.

Re-planning in Traditional Plans is lesser and happens only when changes happen. Re-planning is a norm in Agile Plans as we embrace changes in Agile.

In the Traditional approach, most requirements are known upfront, whereas, on Agile, true requirements emerge as we proceed with the work. Hence, the level of planning also differs accordingly.

Traditional Plans are mostly prepared at the beginning, whereas, Agile Plans are prepared in lumps throughout. This means that we do some high-level planning at the beginning, and then we do detailed planning just before the work is taken up in an iteration. As changes are commonplace on Agile, we re-plan when changes come. In reality, planning in Agile might actually be more than in the traditional approach, as we do it in parts at several times and modify the plan with changes.

Finally, Traditional Plans have few midcourse adjustments as compared to Agile Plans. This is because changes are anticipated more often on Agile.

3.1.1 Minimum Viable Product (MVP)

MVP includes those set of features in the product that help get early customer feedback. All the product features are not needed to get such a feedback. Hence, MVP is only a subset of the total product features that are needed for selling the product. Final product release will have a greater number of features than MVP.

MVP is similar to a mockup or proof of concept, as the purpose is to get customer feedback. With minimal investment, it allows us to check our hypothesis for the product. Similarly, it also helps in validating any critical assumptions taken for the product. This ensures that the final releasable or marketable product has all the required features as expected by the customer.

A good example of MVP is what Airbnb did. They had to prove their hypothesis that people are willing to pay for staying in other people's house. So, they rolled out a basic website for people with at least 3 airbeds and breakfast to list, and for others to rent these. This was their MVP. This helped them confirm their belief and understand what else the customers needed to build the full solution.

3.1.2 Minimally Marketable Product (MMP) / Minimally Marketable Feature (MMF)

Minimally Marketable Product (MMP) or Minimally Marketable Feature (MMF) is the list of those features that form the core functionality of the product. These are the mandatory features that are needed to take the product to the market.

For example, for an ATM machine, the ability to withdraw money from it is its MMP. The ability to allow customized shortcuts to customers to perform their transactions faster, is not an MMP. This is because the product can still be released without the customization feature, which can be added later on in future releases.

Figure 3.2

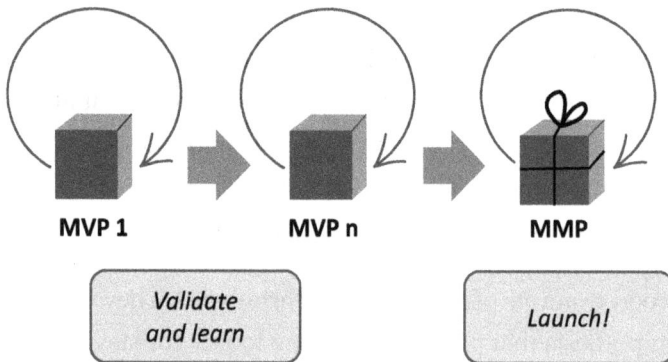

An MVP is not yet ready for selling or for a product release into the market. Only after several MVPs are developed, we reach a stage where we have a saleable product for release. This then becomes a Minimally Marketable Product (MMP) or Minimally Marketable Feature (MMF).

Figure 3.3

Product Backlog

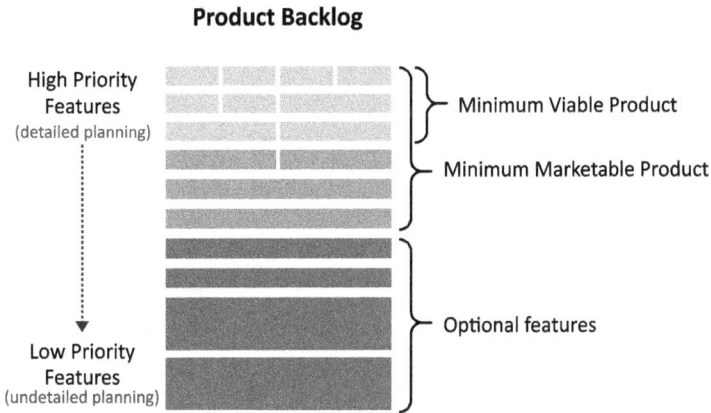

If we look at a Product Backlog that consists of all the product requirements, then some of them could make up the MVP, and when we take a few more, it could make up the MMP. The rest of the requirements are optional, out of which the ones adding more value would eventually be delivered. Several of the optional features might be dropped altogether as per the 80/20 rule – 20% of features provide 80% of value in the product.

3.2 Requirements Gathering

Agile requirements gathering is not a single stage. It happens throughout the lifecycle. In the beginning, a few requirements that are already known are captured and work on them is begun. While the work is carried out, more requirements emerge, and are included in the Product Backlog. Requirements are generally written as User Stories, which are discussed below.

3.2.1 User Stories

User Stories are bite-sized, understandable chunks of business functionality. They are the preferred way of documenting requirements in Agile.

The most commonly used format for making a user story uses three pieces of information - role, functionality, and business benefit. It is written as -

"As a Role, I want Functionality, so that Business Benefit"

As an example, for an eCommerce portal, one of the user stories could be –

"As an Online Shopper, I want to Search for products, so that I can make the right selection"

This format of writing user stories mandates that all user stories should contain business benefit. Hence, it ensures that non-value adding requirements are eliminated.

An alternative format of documenting user stories, especially used for non-functional requirements is –

"Given the pre-condition, when an action is performed by the user, then what is the action taken by the system"

For example –

"Given the user is already registered, when he enters his login-id and password, then he should be logged-in within 3 seconds"

This is an example of a performance requirement of the system.

A user story should always cover all layers of the system architecture, and not just one or a few layers. For example, a user story like "As a User, I want My Name stored in the database, so that I can retrieve it later on", is not a good user story as it mainly covers the database layer. A better user story would be, "As a User, I want to enter my Name in the system, so that it will be available whenever I login to the system".

Figure 3.4

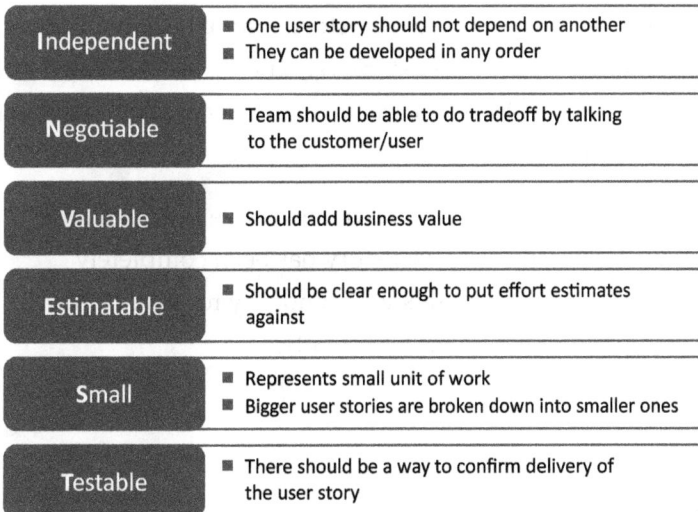

Independent	■ One user story should not depend on another ■ They can be developed in any order
Negotiable	■ Team should be able to do tradeoff by talking to the customer/user
Valuable	■ Should add business value
Estimatable	■ Should be clear enough to put effort estimates against
Small	■ Represents small unit of work ■ Bigger user stories are broken down into smaller ones
Testable	■ There should be a way to confirm delivery of the user story

Effective User Stories should have 6 characteristics called INVEST.

1. **Independent** – Every user story should be independent of other user stories so they can be delivered in any order needed.

2. **Negotiable** – The team should be able to negotiate the functionality of the user story with the users, keeping in mind the time and cost available on the project. The story should not be rigid.

3. **Valuable** – It means that each user story should deliver business benefit.

4. **Estimatable** – Every story should be clear so the team can put effort estimates against them.

5. **Small** – A user story should represent a small unit of work to make it easier to track the work. Bigger stories take more time to deliver and if work is incorrect, it could take costly rework. A user story should be small enough to fit one iteration, as work on a user story cannot be spread across iterations. Bigger user stories should be broken down into smaller ones. We shall see the hierarchy of requirements in the next section.

6. **Testable** – It should be possible to have testcases for confirming that the user story has been completely delivered. Without this we cannot say for sure if the intended delivery has been made.

Figure 3.5

Card	Written on card.
Conversation	Details captured in conversations.
Confirmation	Acceptance criteria confirm that the story is done.

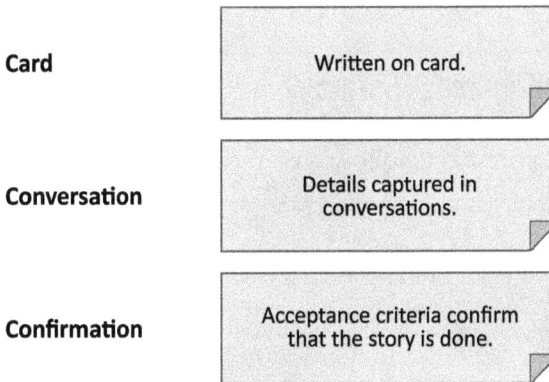

A User Story also has 3Cs associated with it – Card, Conversation, and Confirmation.

1. **Card** – A user story is kept short, so much so that it can be fit on a small card or a sticky note. We purposely do not document too much description of a user story, as we want the development team to communicate with the customer to understand the details.

2. **Conversation** – As a user story is short, conversation between the development team and the customer is expected to happen on a continuous basis. These communications are not to be documented anywhere along with the story. They are only meant for a better understanding of the user stories that helps in their development.

3. **Confirmation** – Each user story should have associated acceptance criteria, which specify the conditions that the deliverables should meet in order for them to be complete.

Acceptance criteria are generally written on the back of the card or sticky note used to write the user story.

3.2.2 Requirements Hierarchy

Agile requirements follow a hierarchy based on the size of the work required to build them.

One of the common hierarchies followed is as shown below.

Figure 3.6

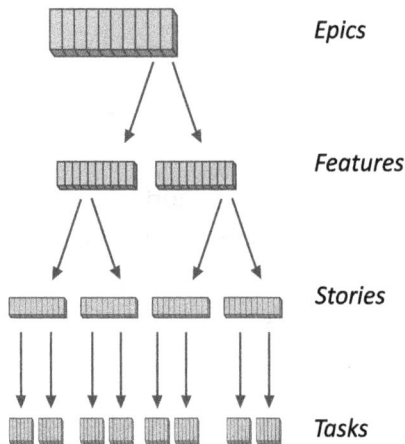

Large user stories are called Epics or Features, which are broken down into User Stories. When a User Story is picked up for development, it may be broken down into Tasks.

All kinds of requirements – Epics, Features, and User Stories, follow the same User Story format we saw earlier.

3.2.3 Remember the Future (Agile Game for requirements elicitation)

The most common way to gather requirements (requirements elicitation) in Agile is by using a fun way – playing a game. A commonly used game is called – Remember the Future.

In this game we invite all stakeholders. Then, we tell them that we are at the end of a successful project + 2 weeks. Next, ask them to list those features that were delivered in the release on sticky notes. We gather all inputs, put them in clusters, remove duplicates, and stick on the wall.

Figure 3.7

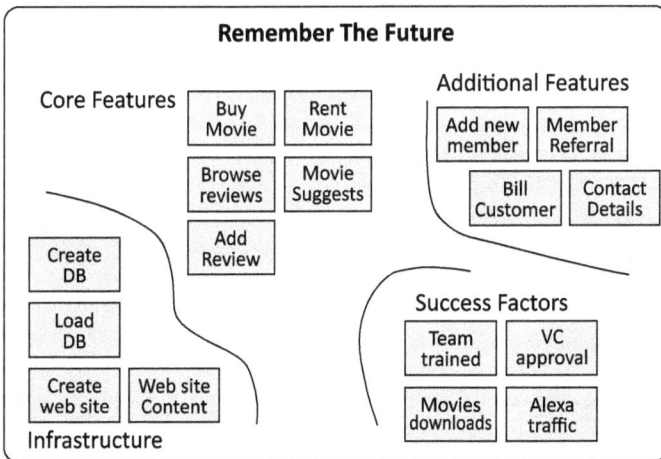

We ask the stakeholders to think they are in future, because as per psychology, we get more accurate results when people think about what happened instead of what should happen.

This game helps in getting better understanding of stakeholder requirements – a requirements elicitation exercise.

3.2.4 Speedboat / Sailboat (Agile Game for risk identification)

Along with the requirements elicitation, we also do risk identification, so that extra risk related requirements can be identified, and it also helps in prioritization of requirements.

In order to do risk identification in Agile in a fun way, we often use the game – Speedboat or Sailboat.

First, draw a sailboat heading towards the shore representing the product. Also draw the waterline and ask the stakeholders to use sticky notes to post opportunities (positive risks) and threats (negative risks) near the boat. Opportunities should be above the waterline and threats below it.

Figure 3.8

This game is used to identify risks – both threats and opportunities.

3.3 Prioritization

We target maximizing value to the customer in Agile. One of the most important ways of doing this is by delivering the most valuable requirements first. To do this, we need to understand the relative priorities of the requirements.

3.3.1 Customer Valued Prioritization

Customer-Valued Prioritization is done by the customer. It is done on the basis of which features add more value to the business.

Those features or requirements that add greater business value are higher on the list and the ones that add lesser value are lower. This helps the development team in deciding the sequence in which features should be built or requirements delivered.

The features or requirements that are lower on the list might be possible candidates for dropping altogether as they add very less business value and it might not be worth investing time and money on delivering them.

Below are some of the common prioritization methods.

Simple Schemes

Figure 3.9

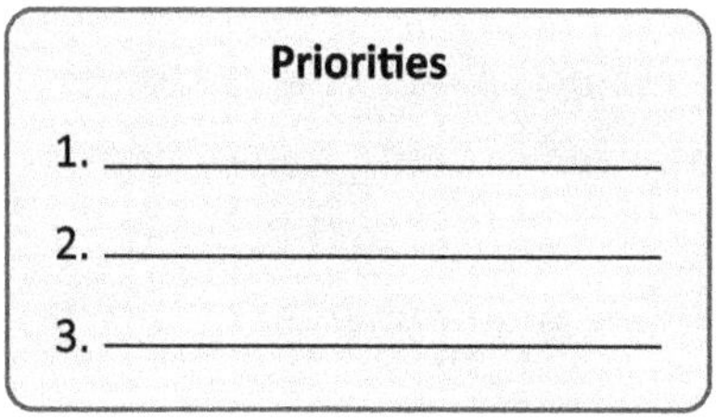

The Simple schemes to do Customer-Valued Prioritization are using a simple linear scale of Priority 1, 2, and 3 or to use High, Medium, and Low. Although this method is easy to understand and use, it sometimes becomes difficult to convince the customer to use lower priorities. Customers would want to give High priority to all or most of the requirements. This makes it difficult to put the requirements in sequence in order to consider them for development.

MoSCoW

In order to avoid customer bias towards high priority, the MoSCoW scheme was developed as part of DSDM Agile methodology. It consists of four priorities based on words rather than numbers of scale.

Figure 3.10

M	**Must have**

• Fundamental feature that should be delivered early

S	**Should have**

• Mandatory feature that can come a little later, but cannot be skipped

C	**Could have**

• Optional feature that adds good value

W	**Would like to have**

• Optional feature that adds very little or no value

M (Must have) – This priority is used against only those features that are fundamental to the system being developed and these have to be delivered in the current timebox only. For example, for development of an online ecommerce portal, being able to see names of items being sold is a Must have feature.

S (Should have) – This priority is used for features that are important for the system to work correctly but can be delivered in a future timebox. For example, for an ecommerce portal, viewing all customer reviews for an item is a Should have feature.

C (Could have) – These features are value adding additions that might be included if time, budget, and resources permit. For example, for an ecommerce portal, being able to see related items often bought together is a Could have feature.

W (Would like to have) – This includes those features that are not so important and will not be delivered at all.

3.3.2 Story Map

Once the user stories have been prioritized, they are placed in a Story Map to get an overall idea about the order of deliveries. Story Maps are generally made on chart papers or whiteboards and displayed in places where all stakeholders can view them.

A Story Map is a pictorial representation of the features that would be included in each release. Story Maps divide user stories into 3 categories based on the features they provide as follows:

1. **Backbone** – Features and epics in the system (high-level user stories)

2. **Walking skeleton** – User stories based on the backbone that are essential parts of the system (Must haves & Should haves)

3. **Other features / Dressing** – User stories based on the backbone that are optional (Could haves & Would like to haves)

Figure 3.11

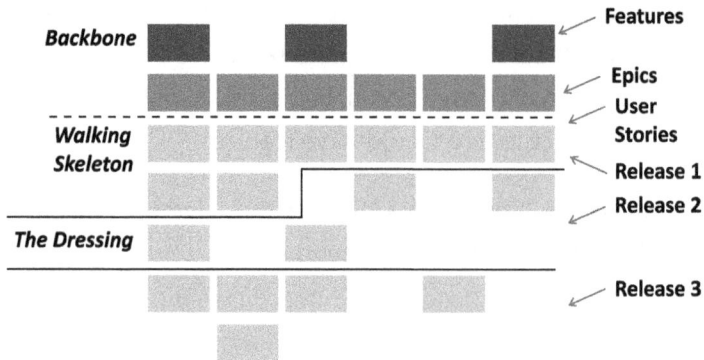

In the above Story Map, we have the top line that consists of Features, which are broken down into Epics on the next line. All of these together make the Backbone. The Epics are further broken down into their constituent user stories that are placed below them in order of their priorities. The ones that are mandatory are a part of the Walking Skeleton, and the optional ones are a part of The Dressing. The user stories are also divided based on which release they will be delivered in – Release 1, Release 2, Release 3, and so on.

3.4 Estimation

Estimation is the process of being able to say how big each user story is, and how long it would take to build, and what would be the building cost.

3.4.1 Relative Sizing / Story Points

It is usually considered difficult to estimate the amount of work on a standalone basis. But it is comparatively easier to do relative estimation. For example, if you are asked to say how much time a particular user story will take to build, it might be difficult to give an answer. However, if you are asked to compare the size of two user stories, it is somewhat easier to come up with a more confident answer.

Figure 3.12

We're pretty good at estimating relatively

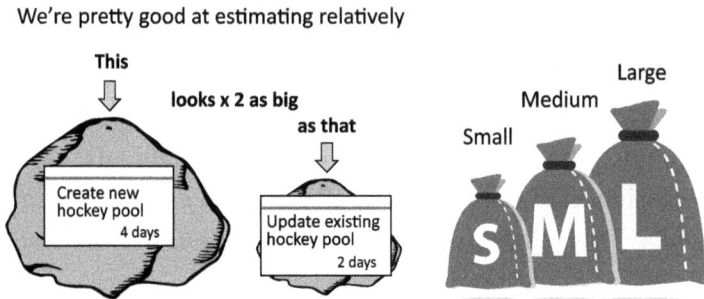

Story Point Estimation is a relative estimation technique where the team estimates a story relative to another story. For this, the team selects a baseline user story, which is generally a small one, and its size is called 1 Story Point. Story Point is a unit that is unrelated to time. It is about the size of the work. For example, 2 story points does not have any relation to the amount of time (unrelated to 2 days or 2 hours) it takes to work on the user story; it is related to the effort required to work on it.

All other user stories on the project are estimated relative to this baseline story. It is like asking, is the work in this user story twice or thrice of the work on the baseline story?

3.4.2 Wideband Delphi

This is a technique used to do relative estimation in Agile.

Figure 3.13

Step 1: Meeting of Group of Experts

We gather a group of experts to discuss the project work. During their meeting, we do the following:

1. The project is broken into details (user stories)

2. Project assumptions and constraints are identified.

3. Boundaries are defined for the project, in order to say what is in scope and what is out of scope. For example, the team might discuss whether documentation is to be included or not.

4. Finally, the acceptable estimation range is agreed upon. This is the tolerance level for the estimation and acts as an exit criterion. For example, the team might agree to a + or – 20% tolerance range.

Step 2: Meeting of Estimators

Once the experts have broken down the project, identified assumptions and constraints, defined boundaries, and estimation tolerance, we hold a kickoff meeting of the estimators to come up with estimates.

The estimators are presented with all the information agreed upon by the experts so far.

Each estimator is asked to provide an anonymous estimate. This avoids any bias in the estimates. This is the round 1 of estimation.

All the estimates gathered in this round are plotted on a graph and shown to everybody to see the spread. If the spread is greater than the agreed estimation tolerance, then a discussion happens on the detailed tasks and assumptions.

Figure 3.14

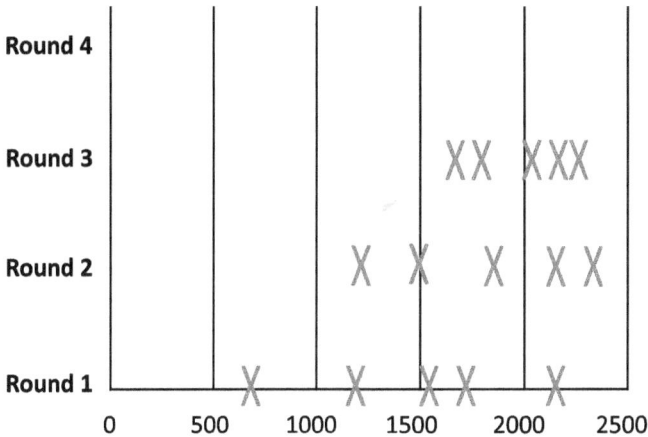

Everybody is asked to re-estimate in round 2 and once again the estimates are plotted on the graph. A comparison is made between the spread of round 2 estimates with tolerance. If we are within the tolerance, then the estimation stops, else we continue to round 3.

Once we have accepted an estimate, detailed list of tasks is documented in a master list.

3.4.3 Planning Poker (Agile Game for Estimation)

Planning Poker is an estimation technique that is a quick implementation of Wideband Delphi. It is quicker, more enjoyable, and uses poker cards.

Figure 3.15

Step 1 of setting the rules of estimation by the group of experts remains the same. During step 2, the estimators are asked to meet face-to-face (or virtually if they are not co-located), and the game is played to do the estimation in real-time. The group is first asked to select a baseline user story – generally the smallest one in the backlog. This user story is given an estimate of 1 story point. Then the estimation starts from the top of the product backlog – one user story at a time.

Generally, the cards used by the estimators to show an estimate follow a Fibonacci sequence that contains 1, 2, 3, 5, 8, 13 and so on. Each person in the estimation meeting is given all the cards from the Fibonacci sequence up to a certain large number (generally no more than 8 or 13). They are asked to use the cards to show their estimate for a particular user story. For example, if an estimator thinks that a particular user story is 5 times as big as the baseline user story, then he selects the card that has a 5 on it.

The moderator reads out the user stories one after the other. The group discusses the user story and then each estimator selects a card for the estimate of the story and keeps it upside down so nobody can see it. Then all the cards are turned at the same time for everybody to see.

If most people have the same estimate, then it is accepted. For example, if three people give an estimate of 5, and one person shows an estimate of 3, then we take the estimate of 5 or an average of all the estimates and continue to the next user story.

But, if one person shows a 13, then there is an outlier, that needs to be discussed and then we go for another round of estimation.

This game continues until all the user stories in the product backlog have been estimated, or at least several high priority user stories have been estimated, or those user stories that have clarity and can be estimated have been estimated, or we have run out of time for the estimation meeting. Estimation is an activity that happens several times as new user stories are added, or some existing user stories become clearer or are modified.

3.4.4 Affinity Estimating (Agile Game for Estimation)

Figure 3.16

1	2	3	5	8	13	21	34

Etc.->

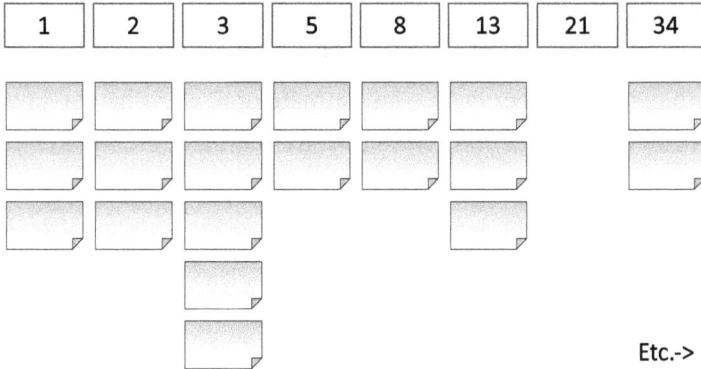

Affinity Estimating is about estimation of story points by putting them in various columns, each representing a size, usually in story points. While doing this estimation, the team is able to see the sizes of the other stories, hence there is a comparison done by the team while estimating the story points. So, this also uses relative estimation method.

We start this method by drawing various columns on the wall. Each column is given a size, like 1 story point, 2 story points, 3 story points, 5 story points etc.

Then each user story is written on a sticky note. Estimators are asked to stick the sticky notes against the correct column that represents the estimate for each user story.

Discussions happen to recalibrate the estimates in order to arrive at the final estimate.

3.4.5 Story Point Estimation Guidelines

Below are some guidelines for Story Point Estimation.

1. **Teams should own the story point definition** – The definition of the size of 1 story point is specific to a team or project. The team decides which story would be the baseline story. We cannot compare story points across teams or projects because the baseline story would be different for each team.

2. **Story point estimates should be all inclusive** – All estimates should include time to build, test, and refactor code.

3. **When disaggregating, the totals need not match** – Sum of detailed estimates of each story might not match with the high-level estimate for its epic story. The detailed estimates are considered more accurate.

4. **Sizes should be relative** – Every user story is estimated using the unit – Story Point, which is relative to the size of the baseline story.

5. **Complexity, work effort, and risks should all count** – Estimation should include all factors, like work complexity, effort, risks, dependencies etc. while estimating.

3.4.6 Ideal Time and Real Time Estimation

When a user story is picked up for delivery in an iteration, it is usually broken down into tasks to make it easy to track. Each task may have a time-based estimate associated to it. When estimating time for each task, we may use Ideal Time Estimation or Real Time Estimation.

We face a lot of interruptions to work, like answering telephone calls, checking email, meetings, and the like. When using Ideal Time Estimation, we inform the team that the entire day (8 hours) is available to perform productive work. We ask them to provide an estimate assuming that there would be no interruptions to work. Using this estimate received from the team member, we calculate duration by factoring in unproductive time. For example, if a team member estimates a work to take 8 hours, then we might convert it to 2 days estimate if only 4 hours a day is actually productive.

On the other hand, when using Real Time Estimation, we inform the team to consider interruptions in their work. Productivity considered would be less than 100%. Hence, we do not need to do any further calculations once the estimate is received from the team. For example, if the productive time is only 6 hours a day, then we ask the team to provide an estimate with that in mind.

Chapter Summary

◆ Planning in Agile happens several times before a piece of work is picked up for development. High-level planning happens early on followed by detailed planning just before the work is picked up for the iteration.

◆ MVP includes the features that are required to get customer feedback about the product requirements. It is not yet ready for selling but is adequate to understand the customers' response. MMP / MMF has all those features that are required to take the product to market.

◆ Requirements are written in the form of user stories, which have three parts – role, functionality, and business benefit. User stories should meet the INVEST characteristics and 3 Cs – Card, Conversation, Confirmation. Large user stories are called Epics.

◆ Requirements gathering can be effectively done using the game – Remember the Future. Risks are identified using the game – Speedboat or Sailboat.

◆ Prioritization of requirements in the product backlog can use simple schemes of 1, 2, 3, or High, Medium, Low. A better technique would be to use MoSCoW – Must have, Should have, Could have, Would like to have. A Story Map shows the features, epics, and prioritized detailed user stories in the product, along with the releases in which the detailed user stories would be delivered.

◆ Estimation is done using relative estimation or story point estimation technique. It provides the size of the work relatively to each other, instead of time units. Wideband Delphi is a technique used to do story point estimation. It could take several rounds of estimation until there is convergence achieved on the estimates. Planning Poker is a quick way to apply Wideband Delphi technique that uses poker cards to show the estimates. Affinity Estimating is an even quicker way to do estimation by putting the user stories in various columns, each representing the size of the user story. All estimation techniques make use of Fibonacci numbers – 1, 2, 3, 5, 8, 13 etc. Story Point estimates should be all inclusive and cannot be compared across teams.

◆ When using Ideal Time estimation, 100% productivity is assumed, whereas for Real Time estimation, less than 100% productivity is assumed during estimation. Ideal Time estimates then need to be converted to time based on actual productivity.

Solved Examples

1. **Which of these correctly describes the difference between MVP and MMP?**

    a. MVP is not deliverable to the end user, whereas MMP is deliverable to the end user

    b. MVP is developing most valuable features first, whereas MMP is developing top marketable features first

    c. MVP is a superset of MMP

    d. MVP is a proof of concept stage, whereas MMP is development of the complete product backlog

Solution:

a. MVP consists of the most basic features that are delivered to the user to get their feedback. MMP consists all the mandatory features to make the product marketable.

2. Which of these is the CORRECT sequence in Delphi technique?

   a. Objectives, round 1, kick-off, discussion, round 2, acceptance

   b. Objectives, kick-off, discussion, round 1, round 2, acceptance

   c. Objectives, kick-off, round 1, round 2, discussion, acceptance

   d. Objectives, kick-off, round 1, discussion, round 2, acceptance

Solution:

d. Wideband Delphi technique uses a group of experts to set the objectives for the estimation, followed by a kick-off of the estimators, and then the various estimation rounds with a discussion in between rounds to clarify estimates and achieve convergence of estimates.

3. **Which of these is NOT a benefit of writing requirements in the form of a user story?**

   a. It makes the customer think about business benefit

   b. It helps in prioritizing user stories later on

   c. It increases interaction between customer and team

   d. It provides implementation-level details

Solution:

d. User stories mandate customer to think about business benefit, as it is a part of the user story format. Due to the presence of the business benefit, later on it makes it easier to prioritize the story as well. Keeping the user story short also encourages greater interaction between the team and the customer, as required in Agile. However, user stories are from the user's perspective, so they do not contain details of implementation.

4. What are the steps in planning in Agile?

Solution:

    i. Writing user stories – can use the game, Remember the Future

    ii. Prioritizing user stories – using MoSCoW technique

    iii. Sizing user stories – using relative estimation / story points using games, Planning Poker or Affinity Estimating

    iv. Estimating iteration tasks – using ideal time or real time estimation

Practice Exercises

1. **Which of these techniques is NOT used for sizing on Agile?**

   a. Remember the Future

   b. Relative Estimation

   c. Story Points

   d. Affinity Estimating

2. **A team is doing sizing using Planning Poker. Three team members show cards with number 3, and two team members show cards with number 13. What should be done?**

   a. Take 13 as the estimate as it is higher

   b. Discuss the details of the user story and go for another round of estimation

   c. Take 13 as the estimate as more team members have gone with it

   d. Take an average of 3 & 13 and take that as the estimate

3. **Which of these is a benefit of using MoSCoW prioritization scheme?**

   a. It is interesting for the customer

   b. It helps the team drop most of the requirements after the prioritization

   c. It helps in estimating the size of each customer requirement

   d. It convinces the customer to correctly prioritize requirements instead of setting all of them to high priority

---

Solutions to the above questions can be downloaded from
the **Online Resources** *section of this book on*
www.vibrantpublishers.com

Chapter **4**

Agile Execution

This chapter includes topics that are related to execution of an Agile project. It discusses how to include risk responses in the product backlog and having spikes for taking care of risks. We discuss various ways to get quick customer feedback and developing with testing in mind. We will also see how Agile contracts are different.

Key learnings:

- How to handle risks in Agile

- How to confirm our understanding of requirements

- How to get early customer feedback on deliverables

- Way to make development a test-driven approach

- Know the various types of Agile contracts

Execution of work in Agile happens in small increments called iterations. Each iteration has the entire lifecycle, from planning to closure. In this chapter, we shall see some of the distinctive elements in the execution stage in Agile.

4.1 Risk Management

Risks are inherent in any work we do. During each iteration planning session, risks are identified, assessed, and responded to by taking appropriate actions. Risk assessment considers two parameters – risk probability, and risk impact. This data proves useful while prioritizing and estimating / sizing work in the product backlog. A high risk for a not so value adding work might push the work lower in priority. Similarly, high risk work may be sized greater, to give time to perform extra risk related actions.

4.1.1 Risk-Based Spike

During the beginning of work, if the team finds that they need to get some more data to assess the risks correctly, then they may request for an iteration specifically to learn more about the risks and ways to mitigate them. This iteration is called a risk-based spike.

A risk-based spike includes development of a proof of concept, that proves that the concept would work, thereby reducing risk. It may be denoted as Iteration 0. A risk-based spike may not deliver any deliverables to the customer, but it could serve a useful purpose of getting a go / no-go decision from the customer.

If, during the risk-based spike, it is found that the concept
is not workable, then a new approach might be needed, or the
venture could be abandoned. As the risk-based spike is taken up
in the early iterations, it allows for "fast failure", that reduces the
amount of loss made on the venture. If a venture is abandoned at a
later time, then the amount of loss would be higher.

4.1.2 Risk-Adjusted Backlog

A Risk-Adjusted Backlog is a single prioritized list containing
the business features and risk responses on the project.

First, the business features of the work are identified, and their
ROI (Return on Investment) is calculated. Prioritization happens
based on the feature ROIs.

Next, the risks on the project are identified and a quantitative
analysis is performed on them by considering their probability of
occurrence and impact. Multiplication of these two values gives us
the Expected Monetary Value or EMV of each risk. Prioritization
of risks is done based on EMV. Risk response actions for some of
the top risks are identified.

Then the two prioritized lists of business features based on ROI
and risk responses based on EMV are joined together to create a
single list called Risk-Adjusted Backlog.

The steps for creating a Risk-Adjusted Backlog are:

1. List all business requirements

2. Calculate their ROI and allocate it to different business
   features to get a prioritized list of business features

3. Identify project risks

4. Identify mitigation responses to risks

5. Calculate EMV for each mitigated risk and put them in a priority list based on EMV

6. Combine both lists to create a single prioritized list containing business features and risk responses

Below is an example of a risk-adjusted backlog.

Figure 4.1

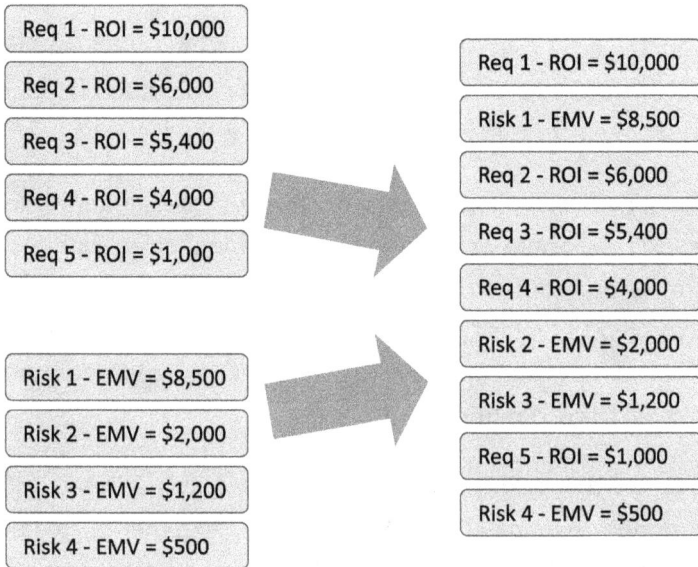

Here is another example of a risk-adjusted backlog that consists of actual requirements of a product, along with risk responses in it. The work items in bold are the risk responses in the risk-adjusted backlog.

Table 4.1

Tasks	Priority
Prepare target audience survey	1
Distribute survey	2
Record survey responses	3
Redistribute survey if insufficient response	**4**
Clarify roles and responsibilities	5
Develop first draft of marketing material	6
Review marketing material	7
Find other reviewers if needed	**8**
Final draft of marketing material	9
Code the website	10
Delays in coding if MySQL can't be used	**11**
Test the website	12
Deploy the website	13

4.2 Prototypes, Simulations, Demonstrations

Confirming that the team is delivering value requires feedback from the customer. For this purpose, we use Prototypes, Simulations, and Demonstrations.

Prototypes are mockups that show the customer how the deliverable would look. As per Agile, we do not want to waste time in less value adding activities. Hence, prototypes are best developed by hand, if possible, instead of wasting time in using a software program. Below is an example of what a prototype in Agile might look like. It also includes customer's feedback in the prototype, kept for future reference.

Figure 4.2

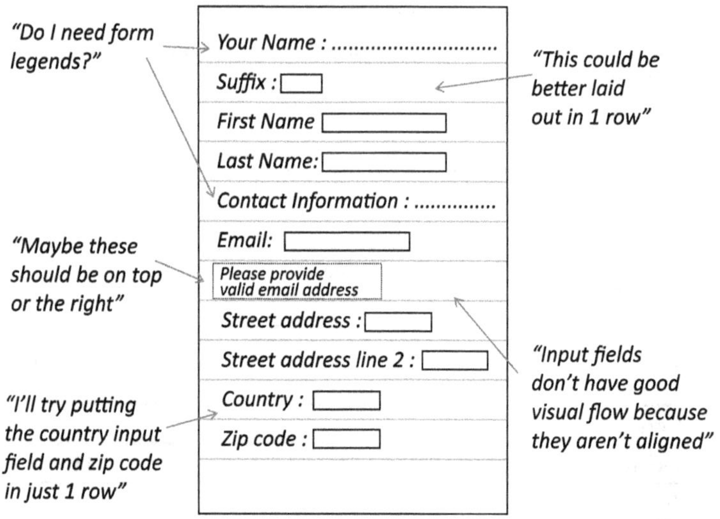

In the above prototype, we see that there are several comments from the customer also being included. This helps the developer understand what exactly the customer needs and refer to this prototype while building the page. This kind of hand-drawn prototypes are simple and quick to create and serve the purpose of getting customer expectations.

Simulations are imitations of the functionality that give the users a feel of the deliverable without actually building it.

Demonstrations are arranged to show the users the features of the product built. They also help in understanding the customers' requirements better. In the process we often get new requirements that were earlier not thought to be important. Demonstrations are done as part of Sprint Review session in Scrum, or a Product Demo session at the end of an iteration.

4.3 Test-Driven Development (TDD) / Test-First Development (TFD)

Test-Driven Development or TDD, also called Test-First Development or TFD, is where test cases are written before developing / coding. This approach helps the developer understand user level functionality and reduce errors while developing.

TDD steps are:

1. Write test cases for the requirement or user story

2. Run test cases, which would all fail as development is yet to be done

3. Develop the requirement or user story

4. Run test cases once again. This time they would pass as development has been done.

Figure 4.3

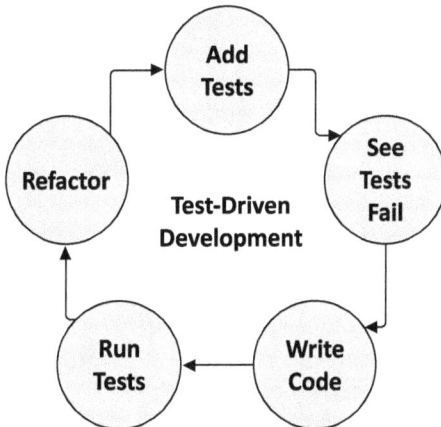

TDD cycle is referred to as Red, Green, Refactor or Red, Green, Clean. Red stands for the first test case run when they fail as development is not yet done. Green stands for the final test case run when they pass as development has been done. After that we either refactor the code or do not perform any further action. Refactoring is rewriting some part of the code to make it easier to understand and maintain without changing the code's behavior.

Figure 4.4

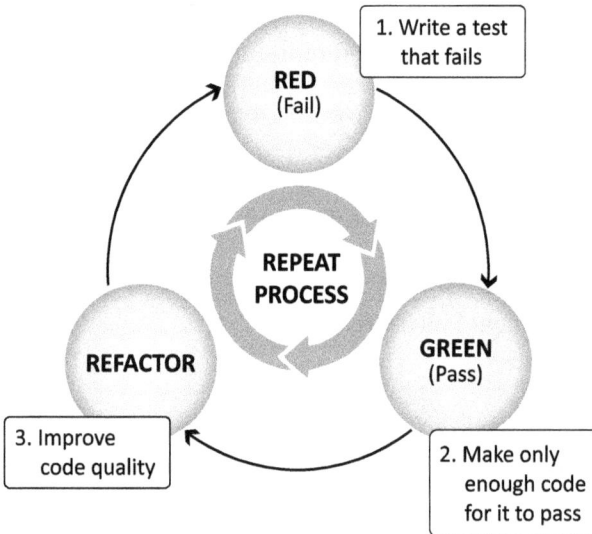

4.4 Acceptance Test-Driven Development (ATDD)

Acceptance Test-Driven Development (ATDD) is based on TDD but instead of unit test cases, these are acceptance test cases that test the user level functionality.

ATDD cycle is as follows:

1. **Discuss** – Discuss the requirements and gather acceptance criteria

2. **Distill** – Distill the tests in framework-friendly format

3. **Develop** – Perform development work and hook up tests

4. **Demo** – Execute tests and show it to the users

Figure 4.5

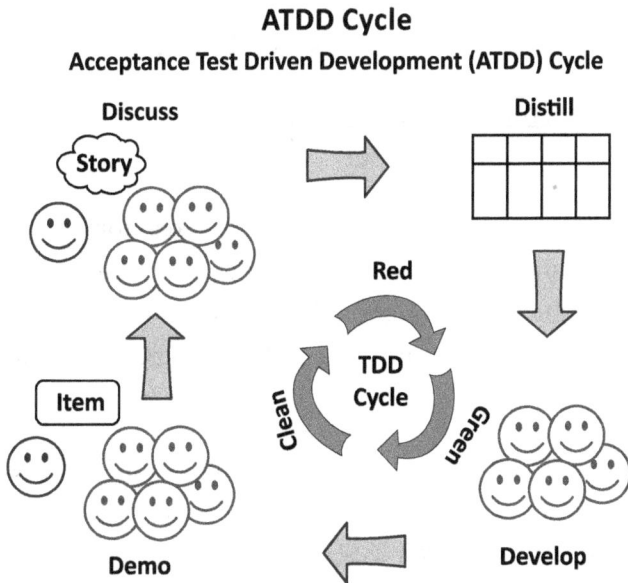

ATDD Cycle
Acceptance Test Driven Development (ATDD) Cycle

4.5 Cycle Time

Cycle Time is a diagnostic measure to see how long it takes to get things done. It is the time for which a particular piece of work is in the process.

Figure 4.6

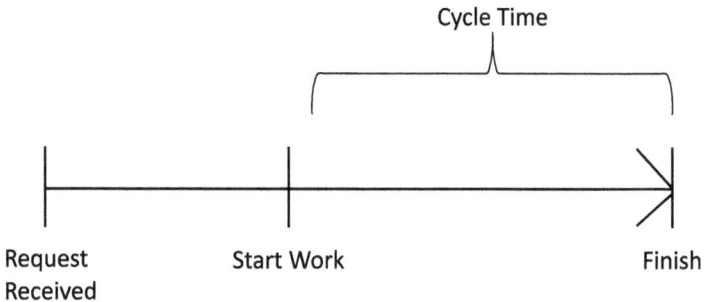

It is measured using Little's Law shown below.

Cycle Time = Work in Progress (WIP)
                            Throughput

Cycle Time is the amount of time work takes from start to finish in the process. WIP is the amount of work at any stage in the process (inventory). Throughput is the number of items delivered or the amount of work completed by the team per unit time, like day, week etc.

For example, let us say the average inventory with the team over the week is 50 story points worth of work, then the WIP = 50. Say, the team delivered 25 story points worth of work over the week, then throughput is 25.

Then the cycle time would be:

Cycle Time = 50 / 25 = 2 weeks

A greater value of WIP leads to delays, as a particular piece of work spends more time in the process.

Cycle Time is a measure that can be used to track cycle time for user stories or to track defects in the team. When calculating cycle time for defects, we get the time between defect injection and defect remediation to see how soon defects are being fixed.

4.6 Escaped Defects

Defects reduce the quality of deliverables and also the customer satisfaction. Several defects may be found while the deliverables are being developed and the team finds a gap. These are fixed before the delivery to the customer. However, some defects might not be caught during this process. These are called Escaped Defects. Escaped Defects are the ones that are found by the customer post-delivery. Escaped Defects are plotted on a graph on an iteration, release, or monthly basis. This shows the trend of these defects that gives an understanding whether we are improving our deliverable quality or not.

In the example graph shown, the Escaped Defects increase in the first five iterations, after which they reduce, probably because the team took some corrective action to bring in greater quality focus or more quality checks.

Figure 4.7

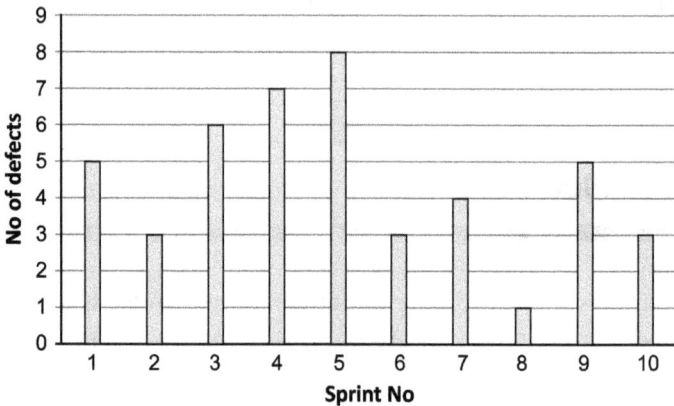

We may also track Escaped Defect Rate or Defect Density by dividing the defects found in an iteration by the number of story points delivered in the iteration. This shows us a trend of defects against the size of the delivery and can be used to compare over time even if the team size changes.

In the example graph shown, we see that the number of story points being delivered are increasing from Sprint 1 to Sprint 7, but the defect density is reducing. This is a good trend.

Figure 4.8

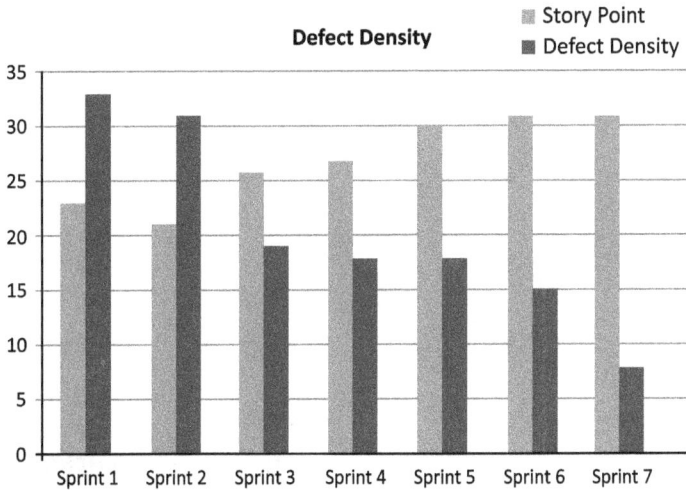

4.7 Agile Contracting

Agile Contracting is different from contracting on traditional work because Agile work has varying scope.

The traditional project triangle has Scope, Time, and Cost, in which the Scope is more static, and Time and Cost vary as per the Scope. Agile uses an inverted form of this triangle where the Time and Resources are fixed, and Scope is variable.

Figure 4.9

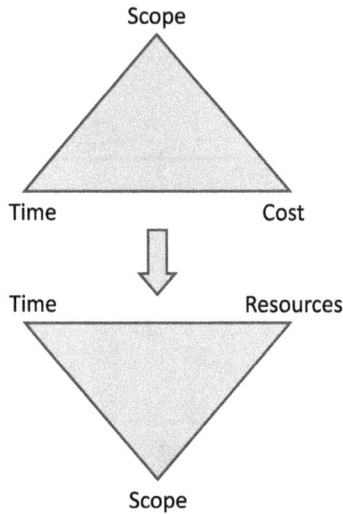

4.7.1 Money for Nothing and Change for Free Contract

One Agile Contracting approach is called Money for Nothing and Change for Free. In this approach, the customer is allowed to make changes and if the new work is of a higher priority, then some other work will be dropped. As long as the total work to be delivered remains the same there is no additional charge. This is called "Change for Free".

This type of contract also has an early termination clause for the customer. After a certain value of the contract has been completed, and the customer feels that the work is no longer adding much value, they can pay a certain amount of the remaining payment and close the contract. This is called "Money for Nothing".

Figure 4.10

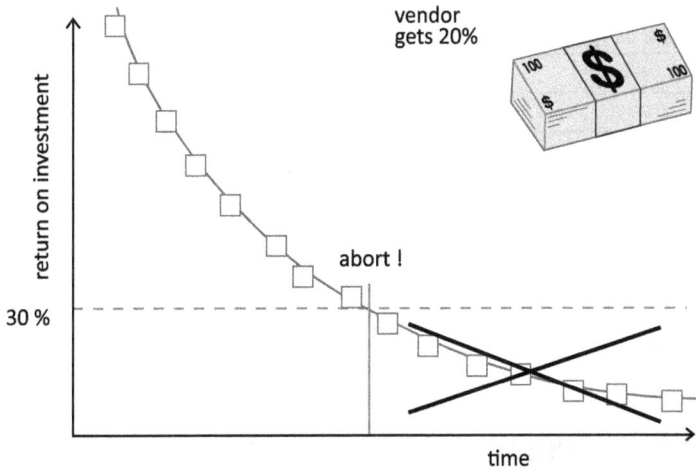

For example, the contract might allow early termination after 70% of the work is completed. In such a case the customer might have to pay only 20% of the remaining contract value in order to close the contract. This gives flexibility to the customer to avoid full payment of the work that does not add much value.

4.7.2 Graduated Fixed Price / Cost Targeted Contract

Another kind of Agile contract is Graduated Fixed Price or Cost Targeted Contract. This contract is based on hourly billing like a Time & Material (T&M) contract. However, the hourly rates differ based on schedule adherence. If the seller delivers early, then they get a higher rate per hour than on-time completion. Similarly, late delivery will give even lower per hour rate to the seller. This provides the seller with an incentive to complete the work earlier.

Table 4.2

Work Completion	Actual Effort	Graduated Rate	Total Fee
Early	800 hours	$110 / hour	$88,000
On Time	1000 hours	$100 / hour	$100,000
Late	1100 hours	$80 / hour	$88,000

As we see in the above table, late deliveries are penalized with a lower hourly rate and early deliveries are rewarded with a higher hourly rate.

4.7.3 Fixed Price Work Packages Contract

Another type of Agile contract is called Fixed Price Work Packages Contract.

As scope varies in Agile, it is difficult to come up with the fixed price contract that includes all the work. Hence, we arrive at a fixed price at a work package or feature level.

This contract also allows the flexibility for change in scope to the customer and re-estimation of remaining work to the seller as new information is available.

Table 4.3

Work Package	Total Fixed Price	Included in Scope
WP1	$10,000	Yes
~~WP2~~	~~$5,000~~	~~No~~
WP3	$25,000	Yes
WP4	$7,000	Yes
Total Price	$42,000	

In the above example, a price is calculated for each work package and not for the entire scope of work. This gives flexibility to the customer to remove any work package from the scope, without doing any calculation. Total price will be determined based on which work packages are delivered.

Chapter Summary

◆ A Risk-Based Spike is also called iteration 0. It is taken up to perform work that reduces the overall risk of the work. It may lead to pre-mature closure of the venture if risks are found to be unacceptable. A Risk-Adjusted Backlog combines user requirements and risk mitigation actions with relative priorities.

◆ Prototypes are to be developed quickly to get alignment with customer's requirements. Simulations may be used to show the customer how the output would look. Demonstrations are done after the deliverables are ready.

◆ TDD or TFD is a concept of writing test cases before development. This ensures that the developer concentrates only on the user's requested functionality. ATDD is an extension of TDD but applies to the acceptance tests that the user uses to accept team's deliveries.

◆ Cycle Time is a diagnostic measure that tells us how much time work takes to go through the various process stages. In order to keep cycle time low, WIP (Work In Progress) needs to be reduced. Escaped Defects are the defects passed on to the customer.

◆ Agile Contracts are more flexible on scope. They allow for scope changes by replacing work of equal size, having fixed price work packages instead of fixed sized project, allowing early termination clause, and incentivizing early deliveries.

Solved Examples

1. **Iteration 0 is taken up for the purpose of -**

   a. Planning

   b. Business case development

   c. Cost reduction

   d. Risk reduction

Solution:

d. Iteration 0 is often called a risk-based spike, taken up to try out a solution that helps in risk reduction.

2. **On an Agile project, the WIP is 5 items and the delivery in the iteration is 10 story points per week. What is the Cycle Time?**

   a. 2.5 days

   b. 0.5 days

   c. 3 days

   d. 3.5 days

Solution:

a. Cycle Time = WIP / Throughput = 5 / 10 = 0.5 week = 2.5 days.

3. What is the benefit of having WIP limits?

a. Speeds up delivery

b. Ensures that all team members are fully utilized

c. Assists in accepting changes in scope

d. Removes all slack from the work

Solution:

a. WIP limit ensures there are lesser partial deliveries and less task switching. This helps speed up deliveries. As per Little's Law, Cycle Time = WIP / Throughput. Hence, as WIP reduces, Cycle Time also reduces.

4. What are the benefits of using TDD and ATDD?

Solution:

TDD and ATDD base the development on test cases written instead of the other way around. It has the following benefits:

i. Greater focus on actual deliverables

ii. Lower chances of extra deliveries

iii. Better understanding of user requirements before starting to develop

iv. Clear understanding of how the user will provide sign-off of the deliverables

Practice Exercises

1. **A risk-adjusted backlog consists of –**

   a. User stories based on EMV and risk responses based on ROI

   b. User stories based on ROI

   c. User stories based on ROI and risk responses based on EMV

   d. Risk responses based on EMV

2. **Which of these is the correct sequence in TDD?**

   a. Write tests, write code, perform testing, refactor

   b. Write code, write tests, perform testing, refactor

   c. Write code, write tests, refactor, perform testing

   d. Write tests, perform testing, write code, perform testing

3. **Which of the following is NOT a difference between regular contracts and Agile contracts?**

   a. Agile contracts are more flexible

   b. Agile contracts do not need change control section as changes are a normal occurrence

   c. Agile contracts provide more flexibility for early termination

   d. Agile contracts may have fixed price work packages instead of a fixed price for the project

---

Solutions to the above questions can be downloaded from
the **Online Resources** *section of this book on*
www.vibrantpublishers.com

Chapter 5

Agile Tracking and Reporting

This chapter discusses the various preferred communications methods in Agile. The different charts and graphs that are commonly used in Agile are included in this chapter. We also see how to track schedule and cost in Agile.

Key learnings:

- Communications methods used in Agile

- Charts used during iterations and across iterations to share status with stakeholders

- Schedule and cost tracking technique

Communication, tracking, and reporting in Agile is far more informal compared to the traditional approach. For example, there are no formal weekly reports sent to the stakeholders. Instead, dynamic, real-time reports are picked up directly by stakeholders from pre-determined places (a wall, chart papers on a wall, whiteboards, or software tools, like Jira). These real-time reports are updated by the team as they produce their deliverables.

5.1 Agile Communications

In Agile, the most preferred way to communicate is face-to-face communication. However, it might not be always possible to have this kind of communication. But it is used whenever available.

Figure 5.1

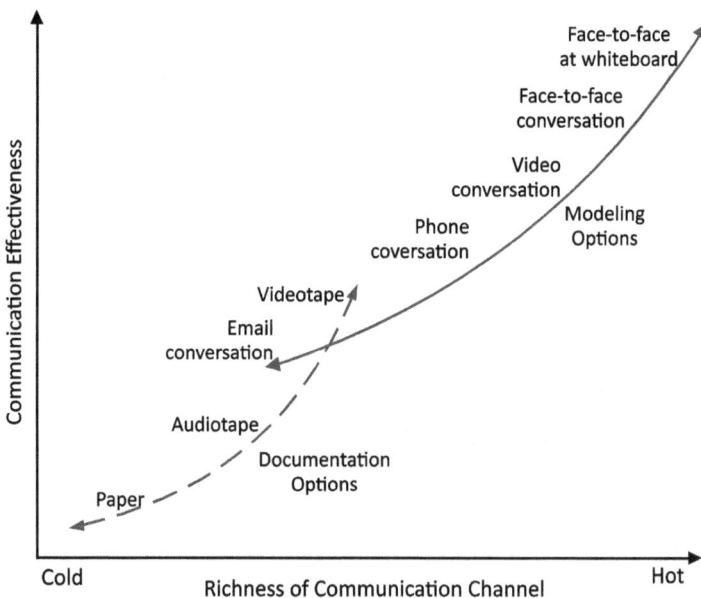

As seen in the above Communication Effectiveness diagram, the communication effectiveness and communication richness or temperature depends on the medium of communication used. It is plotted for two-way communication as well as one-way communication.

For two-way communication, face-to-face discussion using a whiteboard is the most effective, followed by just face-to-face discussion, video, audio, and emails.

For one-way communication, the most effective way is seeing a video, followed by audio, and then paper based.

5.2 Information Radiators

Information Radiator is a term that encompasses several different items. It is an umbrella term that refers to all highly visible ways to display work information.

They are in the form of large charts, graphs, or summaries of work data. For example, a graph showing the number of defects found over a period of time, maybe last several iterations, is an Information Radiator.

Below is an example Information Radiator showing a blend of graphical data.

Figure 5.2

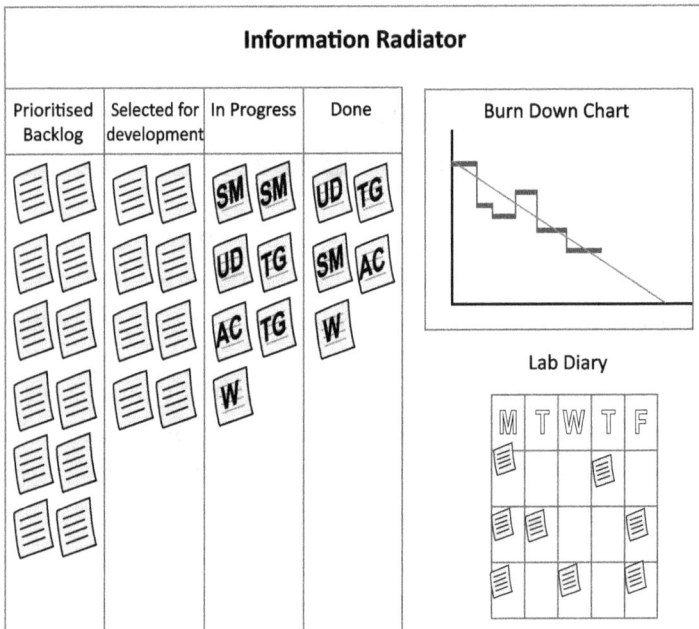

Information Radiators are generally placed on walls near the team's work area that are high-traffic areas. This ensures maximum exposure as everyone who passes from that area will be able to view them. They help providing an updated status to all stakeholders.

The charts and graphs that are usually included in an Information Radiator are described in the next few sections – Burndown Chart, Burnup Chart, Cumulative Flow Diagram, Velocity Chart, and Kanban / Task Board.

5.2.1 Burndown Chart

Burndown Charts are one of the most commonly used Agile communication tools.

A Burndown chart is drawn with effort remaining on the Y-axis and time on the X-axis for a particular iteration. There are two lines on the chart, one showing the ideal effort remaining and the other showing the actual effort remaining. Depending upon how the two lines are going in relation to each other, we can say whether we are on-time, late, or early. Below is an example.

Figure 5.3

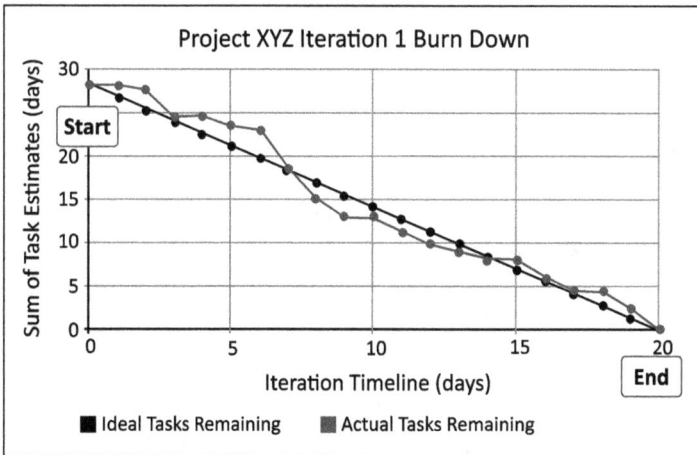

Project XYZ Iteration 1 Burn Down

In the diagram, we see that the straight line shows ideal effort remaining and the zig-zag line shows actual effort remaining. In the first few days of the iteration, we are falling late as more actual effort is remaining as compared to ideal effort remaining, until around day 7. After this, the work starts happening faster and we are ahead until day 14. The two lines finally coincide on day

20. When the actual effort remaining line reaches zero, we have completed the work for the iteration.

Burndown chart can also be drawn by using estimated story points remaining against time.

One major drawback of a burndown chart is that if there is a change of scope for the iteration, then we shall see a slower burndown of the actual work. The chart will not differentiate the slowdown reason. It can be due to reduction of productivity or due to additional scope. We cannot tell the difference.

5.2.2 Burnup Chart

A Burnup Chart is the opposite of a Burndown Chart. It plots story points completed against time, or iterations.

Figure 5.4

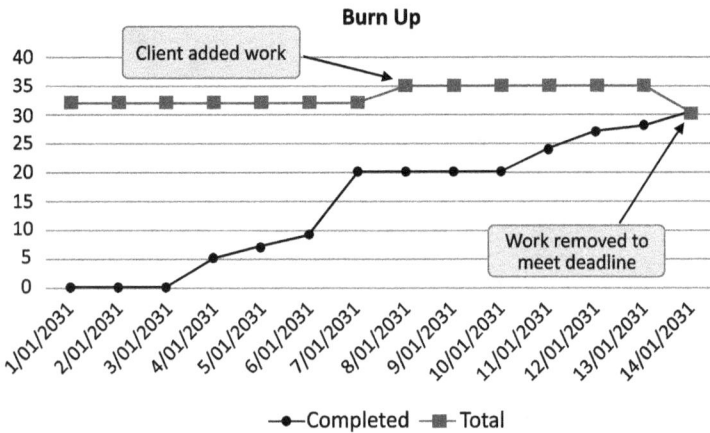

In the burnup chart above, we see story points delivered (work completed) being plotted against dates. In the above example, the first delivery happens from fourth day onwards, and then we keep adding more deliveries cumulatively to it.

A burnup chart also shows the total scope line that goes up or down if scope changes. This is an advantage of burnup chart over burndown chart. It clearly shows a change in scope. When the work done line meets the total scope line, all the work is completed, and there is no story pending.

5.2.3 Cumulative Flow Diagram (CFD)

Cumulative Flow Diagram or CFD is a useful tool to track and forecast progress.

A CFD is an extension of the Burnup Chart seen earlier. The only additional data to be shown is the in-progress work. A CFD is drawn using the total features, in-progress features, and completed features over time. It shows how the team is progressing over time.

Figure 5.5

☐ Not Started ☐ Started ☐ Completed

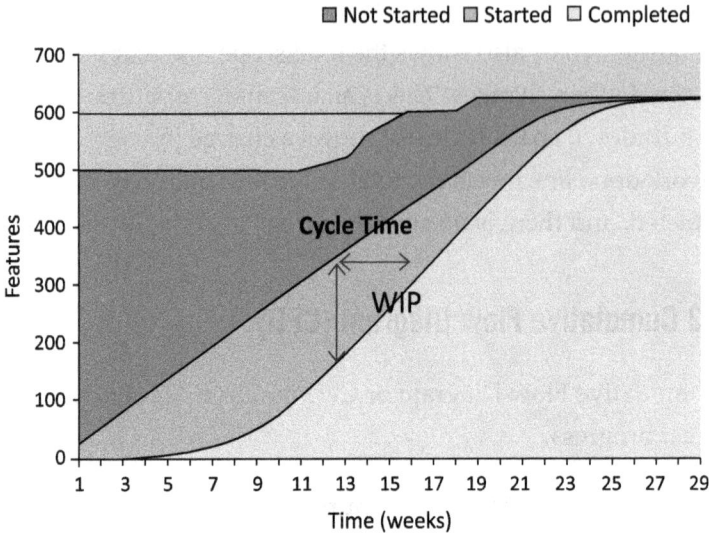

In the CFD shown above, there are three lines plotted, thereby creating three different bands. Two of the lines drawn are the same as in the burnup chart – total scope (topmost line) and work completed (bottommost line). An additional line for work in progress is also drawn (the one in between). This creates three areas in the diagram (from top to bottom) – work pending, work in progress, and work completed.

It can also be used to calculate the cycle time and work in-progress or WIP. Cycle Time is the amount of time it takes to complete a feature. It is calculated by looking at the width of the in-progress features band on the diagram. WIP is the amount of in-progress features in the system at any point of time. This is given by the height of the in-progress features band on the diagram. These values are useful in estimating the number of features that can be delivered in an iteration.

5.2.4 Velocity Chart

Velocity is an important parameter tracked in Agile. It describes the team's capacity to perform work in an iteration. It can be measured either in story points delivered or hours or days of efforts put.

Velocity is tracked across iterations and the velocity of the previous iterations is used in order to estimate the amount of work that can be taken up in the future iterations.

Figure 5.6

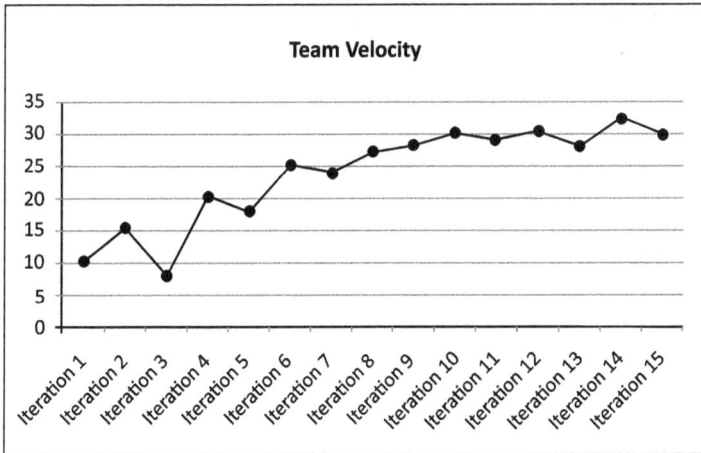

In a team, the initial velocity would be lower as the team gets used to working together in the beginning. Then it rises steadily and reaches a peak, beyond which it flattens. This is because improvements have an upper limit and then there is little scope of further improvement.

When calculating Velocity, we only account for work that is completed. Any work that is partially completed, is not counted at all in calculating velocity. For example, if we have completed work worth 10 user stories completely in the iteration and work worth 5 user stories partially, the velocity of the iteration would be 10. Partially completed work will not be accounted for at all. Hence, we are using a tracking system that has only two states - 0% completion and 100% completion. Partial completion is shown as 0% only.

5.2.5 Kanban / Task Board

We have already looked at a Kanban or Task Board. It is a low-tech, high-touch tool used in Agile that is simpler to understand than Gantt Charts used in the traditional approach. It is used to clearly display what the current work status is to all stakeholders.

Figure 5.7

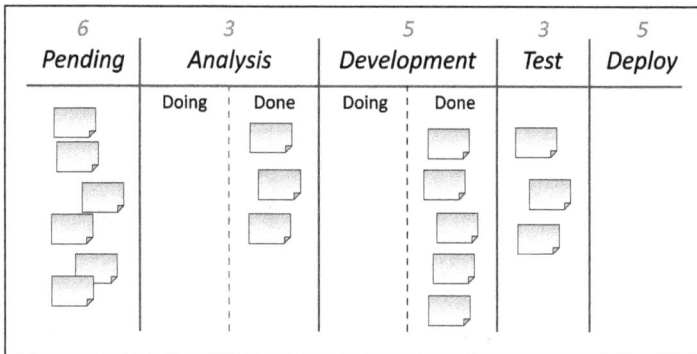

A Kanban Board can be drawn on a whiteboard or chart paper and stuck on the wall. But, if the stakeholders are at different physical locations, then it is drawn using tools, like Jira and Trello.

5.3 Agile Earned Value Management (EVM)

On Agile, the Earned Value Management technique is used to show graphical views of work progress instead of the various calculations in numerical form, because graphs and charts are easier for stakeholders to understand than raw numerical data.

Schedule tracking parameter that is tracked is called Schedule Performance Index or SPI. This is calculated by dividing story points delivered by story points planned.

SPI = <u>Story Points Delivered</u>
    Story Points Planned

SPI < 1 means behind schedule

SPI = 1 means on schedule

SPI > 1 means ahead of schedule

Figure 5.8

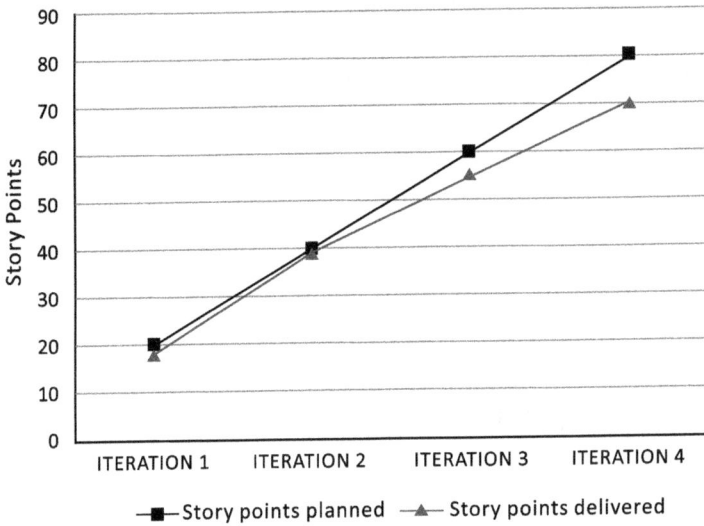

The graph above shows the SPI over iterations. It shows the planned story points against delivered story points per iteration. We see in the graph that the delivered story points are less than the planned story points. Hence, the team is running behind schedule. For calculating SPI for iteration 4, we would do the following:

SPI = 70 / 80 = 0.875

It means that we are running at 87.5 percent of the planned schedule.

Cost tracking parameter that is tracked is called Cost Performance Index or CPI. This is calculated by dividing planned cost of story points delivered by actual cost incurred so far.

CPI = <u>Planned Cost of Story Points Delivered</u>
                  Actual Cost Incurred

CPI < 1 means spending is more than planned

CPI = 1 means spending is as planned

CPI > 1 means spending is less than planned

Figure 5.9

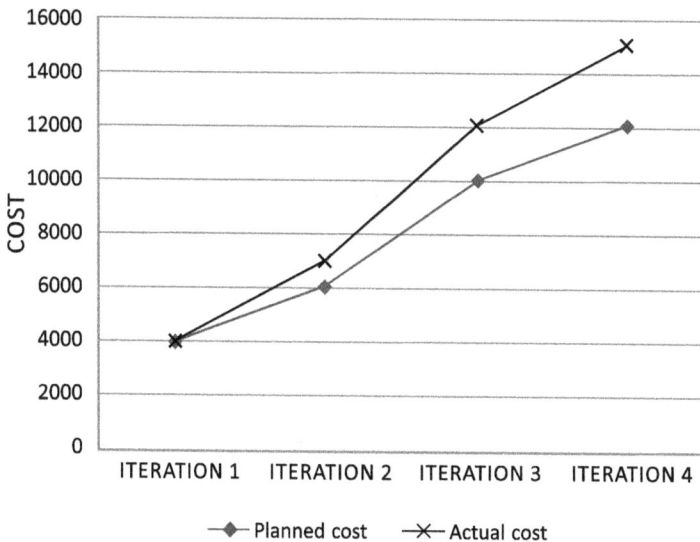

This graph shows the planned and actual costs per iteration. We see that there is a cost overrun by the team. While tracking in Agile, we consider only those story points that have been 100% delivered or done. Partially completed story points are not counted at all. So, we use a scale of either 0% or 100%. No partial completion percentage is used.

CPI for iteration 4 can be calculated as:

CPI = $12,000 / $15,000 = 0.8

It means that for every dollar being spent, we are getting deliverables worth only 80 cents.

Chapter Summary

◆ Preference is given to face-to-face communication in Agile. It is the most effective way of communicating.

◆ Information Radiators is a collective term, that includes any information that could be shared with the stakeholders to show them the work status.

◆ A Burndown Chart shows work remaining in an iteration. A Burnup Chart shows work done over unit time (based on dates or iterations). A Cumulative Flow Diagram shown the work done, work in-progress, and work pending over unit time. It can be used to know cycle time and WIP. A Velocity Chart shows the team's productivity over iterations. A Kanban Board shows the status of each piece of work in the iteration.

◆ Agile EVM has two terms – SPI and CPI, that we track. SPI tells us where we are against schedule. CPI tells us how our spending is against plan. Both, SPI and CPI, are shown in a graphical form.

Solved Examples

1. Which of these is a feature of a Burndown chart?

   a. It does not show scope changes

   b. It shows hours spent per iteration

   c. It shows how product backlog is prioritized

   d. It shows amount of work completed so far

Solution:

a. A burndown chart cannot differentiate between low productivity and scope changes. It shows work remaining in the iteration.

2. Which of these is NOT a use of tracking Velocity?

    a. It can be used to decide what goes in the iteration

    b. It can be used to decide the number of iterations needed

    c. It can be used to see if the team has reached a stage of maximum possible productivity

    d. It can be used to show scope changes on the project

Solution:

d. Velocity is the amount of work done in an iteration. This value helps in committing work for the next iteration, and to know how many iterations would be needed to finish all the work. As the work progresses, velocity reaches a peak, when productivity is the highest. However, velocity does not have any relation to scope changes.

3. What is the purpose of Information Radiators?

Solution:

Information Radiators is a collective term that includes any work information shared with the stakeholders. It generally includes charts and graphs, line Burnup Chart, Burndown Chart, Kanban Board, and Velocity Chart.

A Kanban Board shows detailed work status in the process, Burndown Chart shows work remaining in the iteration, Burnup Chart shows work done, and Velocity Chart shows the team's capacity to do work (productivity).

Practice Exercises

1. **Cumulative flow diagram, Burnup chart, and Burndown chart are all examples of -**

   a. Information refrigerators

   b. Agile modeling tools

   c. Information radiators

   d. Lean tools

2. **During the iteration planning meeting, the Agile team is discussing the tool that they should use for showing current work status. Which of the below tools would be useful to share project status with the stakeholders?**

   a. Product backlog

   b. Kanban board

   c. Story board

   d. Product roadmap

3. **If SPI for the team is 1.2, it means -**

    a. The team is spending more money than planned

    b. The team is spending less money than planned

    c. The team is behind schedule

    d. The team is ahead of schedule

Solutions to the above questions can be downloaded from
the **Online Resources** *section of this book on*
www.vibrantpublishers.com

This page is intentionally left blank

Chapter **6**

Agile Project Management

This chapter covers the various characteristics of Agile teams and their work locations. It also talks about what an Agile leader does at the different stages in an Agile team.

Key learnings:

- Agile team characteristics and how to achieve them

- Understanding of Agile team's workplace

- Leadership in Agile and the leader's characteristics

- Changes to leadership style based on team development stages

Project Management in Agile is different from the traditional management approach, as it is more about leadership and assistance from the leader, than decision making. A lot of the traditional manager's power are passed on to the team.

6.1 Agile Team Characteristics

The two most important characteristics of Agile teams are that they are self-organizing and self-directing.

6.1.1 Empowered Team

Empowered teams are those teams that are self-organizing and self-directing. Agile teams need to be empowered.

Self-organizing teams are free from command-and-control management. They are free to do the work as they deem right. They get all the support they need from the servant leader.

Self-directing teams create collective team norms or rules and also make their own local decisions. They are also collectively accountable for the team's success or failure.

6.1.2 High-performance Team

A Team is defined as "A small number of people who carry complementary skills, and are committed to a common purpose and have the same performance goals, and who hold themselves mutually accountable for the goals"

In order to create a high-performance team, we need to:

1. Create a shared vision for the team so that the team is committed to achieve it

2. Set realistic goals so the team manages to achieve it

3. Limit the team size to 12 or less to ensure that there is communication between all team members. Small teams also have greater bond between them.

4. Build a sense of team identity by giving collective ownership for deliverables

5. Provide strong leadership so that the servant leader can provide all the support that the team needs to succeed

Motivation is critical in building a high-performance team. Motivation is an internal good feeling that one has about the work the person is performing. This increases the person's productivity.

All team members should be aligned or motivated towards the team's goal to ensure that the net effect is to reach the goal. If any team member is not properly aligned to the team's goals, then it may lead to a failure.

Alignment of all team members to the team's goals can be done by aligning the team members' personal goals with those of the team. Once they are all aligned, they would be highly motivated to achieve the team's goals and increase chances of success of the team.

For example, if team members are looking to learn a new domain being implemented in the team, a training could be arranged for them. This ensures that they learn the new skills they want, and, at the same time, the team benefits from their enhanced knowledge. It is a win-win situation.

6.1.3 Team Space

Team Space is the term used for the designated environment

used by the Agile team members to conduct their everyday work.

In Agile, it is preferred to have all the team members sitting at the same place, called co-location or war room. This area should also have plenty of wall space to write or stick information radiators.

Figure 6.1

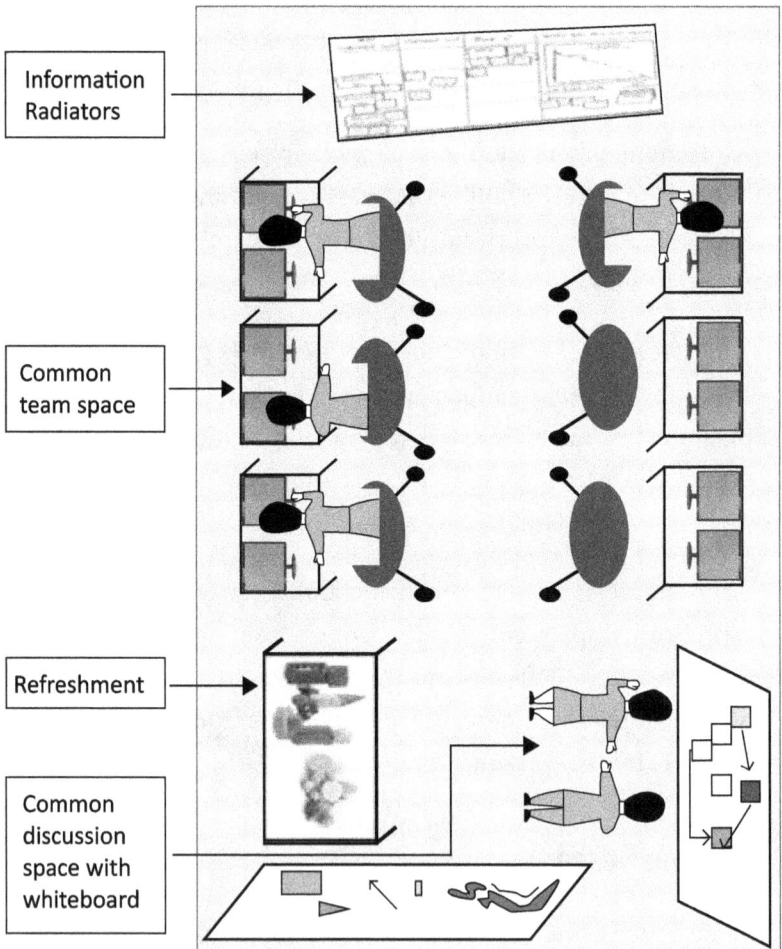

In the above diagram of an Agile team space, we see that the team members are co-located, with common space for discussion using a whiteboard, space for information radiators, and lots of refreshments, for the team's convenience.

6.1.4 Co-located & Distributed Team

Co-location means that the entire team sits at the same place. This is the preferred mode of working in Agile. There are two types of work areas used in Agile co-location – Caves and Common.

Common refers to the team's work area where all team members sit. Caves refer to a private place that individual team members can use in order to take personal calls, do private work, or go to for a short period of isolation.

Private booths shown below are an example of a cave.

Figure 6.2

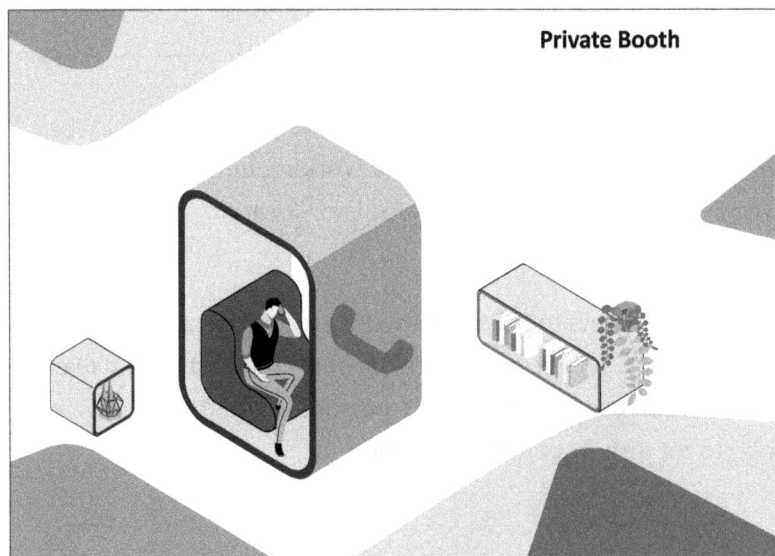

Co-located teams have two communication benefits shown – Osmotic Communication and Tacit Knowledge.

Osmotic Communication means that somebody overhears your conversation. If team members are co-located, then all of them are in hearing distance. This can help them pick up some critical information that can avoid conflicts. For example, if two team members are talking about an upgrade, another team member may point out that it should be done after 2 days, as they are yet to complete some critical features.

Tacit Knowledge is information that is not written down. It is there with the individual team members and can be used if they are co-located. For example, if somebody wants to know how to use a certain feature of an application, he can simply ask aloud, as everyone is in earshot, and he might be able to get an answer.

Sometimes, Agile teams may not be co-located. They might be physically separated from each other. This is referred to as a Distributed Team. Even if one team member works remotely, it becomes a distributed team.

When there is a distributed team, it is best to spend on team's travel in the early phase of work to improve communication. It is recommended to conduct iteration planning, iteration review, and retrospective meetings using face-to-face communication.

Using tools like Videoconferencing, instant messaging, and interactive whiteboards helps to improve communication effectiveness in a distributed team.

6.2 Agile Leadership

Leadership in Agile is more about coaching, mentoring, and facilitating than directing. A traditional Manager tells the team what to do, how to do, and tracks their performance. This is called command-and-control management. All of these functions are passed on to the team in Agile, thereby empowering them. The Agile Leader takes on the job of ensuring that there is no hindrance to the team's progress.

6.2.1 Adaptive Leadership

Figure 6.3

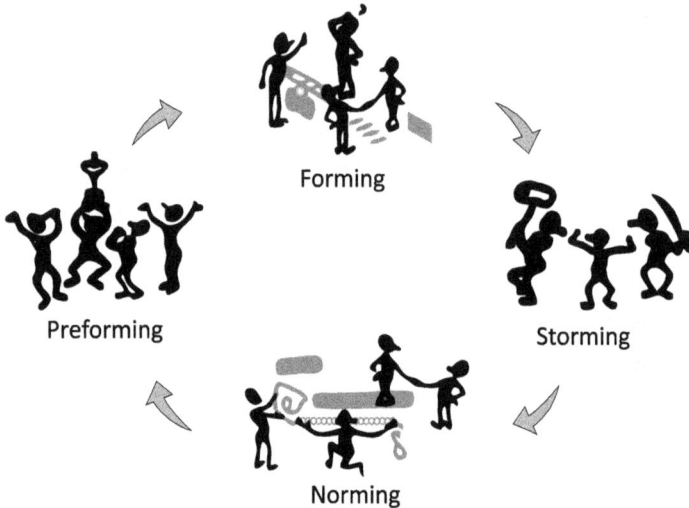

Forming

Storming

Norming

Preforming

A team goes through 5 stages of development:

1. **Forming** – The team is formed when the team members
   join the team. At this stage, it is just a working group that is
   learning about each other.

2. **Storming** – The team sees a lot of conflicts as the team
   members are not yet acquainted with each other. This is a
   pseudo team with conflicts.

3. **Norming** – The conflicts reduce as the team members start
   knowing each other better and are able to complement their
   skills. This is a potential team that now understands each
   other.

4. **Performing** – The team starts working productively to achieve the team's objectives. This is now a real team that works together as a single unit.

5. **Adjourning** – The team is released once the work is done.

The stages of storming, norming, and performing are iterative due to changes in team structure. In Agile, we may make changes to the team only at the end of an iteration.

As the team development goes in stages, the leadership style to manage the team also changes as per the stage. This is called situational leadership.

Figure 6.4

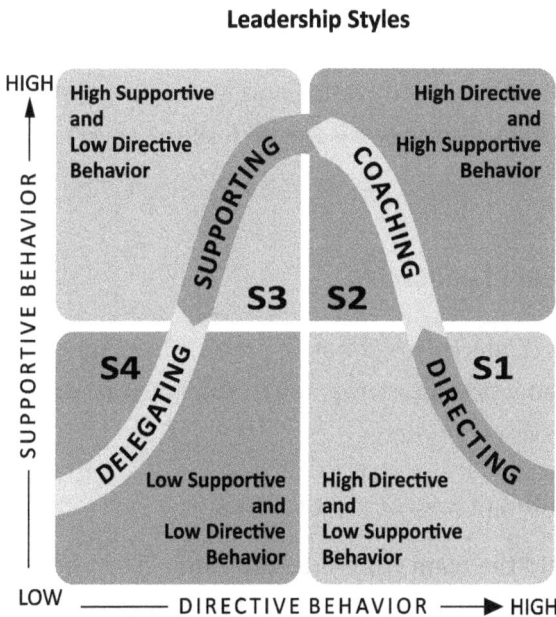

Leadership Styles

When the team is being formed and is in the early stages of development, the leadership style that is most appropriate is called Directing. In this style, the leader gives several directions to the team. The team at this stage expects more directions and less support from the leader. This is when the leader is driving the team. This is the Forming stage of team development.

As the team matures, the leadership style changes as the team now starts performing some jobs on their own and along with directions also expects high support from the leader. This is termed as Coaching. This is the Storming stage of team development.

With further maturity of the team, they need lesser direction and greater support. This stage is called Supporting. It is the Norming stage of team development.

Finally, once the team is fully mature, the leader starts to delegate work in a low directing and low support environment. This is called Delegating. It is the Performing stage of team development.

6.2.2 Servant Leadership

Servant Leadership is the style practiced by Agile leaders. In this, the leader acts as a servant to the team in order to ensure that the work goes on smoothly.

Primary duties of a servant leader are:

1. **Shield the team from interruptions** – The leader needs to ensure that the team is focused on value-adding work and does not get distracted by constantly changing work items.

2. **Remove impediments to progress** – The leader helps remove any roadblocks to the team's work.

3. **Communicate or re-communicate vision** – The leader should communicate the vision to the team at every opportune moment to ensure that the team stays focused.

4. **Provide essential resources** – The leader should ensure that everything that the team needs is made available to them. This also includes human resource practices of celebrations, trainings, rewards, and recognitions.

Traits of a good leader are:

1. **Honesty** – A leader should be transparent and open to build trust

2. **Forward-looking** – The leader should share the vision of the team

3. **Competent** – The leader should be able to understand the work at a high-level, so as to avoid being a liability to the team

4. **Inspiring** – The leader should display enthusiasm and team spirit to motivate the team

Chapter Summary

◆ Agile teams are empowered, which is because they are self-organizing and self-directing. To build a high-performance team, there needs to be shared vision, realistic goals, small team size, strong team identity, and strong leadership.

◆ A co-located team space consists of work area called Common and private area called Cave. Co-location assists in Osmotic communication and Tacit knowledge. Osmotic communication is about gathering knowledge from the neighborhood. Tacit knowledge is the unwritten knowledge available with people. Distributed team needs to make use of communication technology.

◆ A team goes through 5 stages of development – forming, storming, norming, performing, and adjourning. Adaptive leadership is about the leader changing his leadership style to adjust to the stages of team's development. It starts with directing, then coaching, followed by supporting, and finally delegating.

◆ An Agile leader is a servant leader who shields the team from interruptions, removes impediments in their way, constantly communicates the vision, and provides all essential resources for them to work effectively. An Agile leader should be honest, forward-looking, competent, and inspiring.

Solved Examples

1. **During which team development stage does the leader need to do conflict management the most?**

   a. Norming

   b. Forming

   c. Storming

   d. Performing

Solution:

c. Storming is the stage when conflicts in the team are the most. To reach the Performing stage, these conflicts need to be reduced, and the leader could play a vital role in assisting the team to reduce conflicts.

2. **Which of these describes Osmotic Communication?**

   a. Information gathered due to relationship

   b. Information gathered from neighborhood

   c. Asking aloud to get information

   d. Verbal communication

Solution:

b. Osmotic communication happens when a team is co-located, and all team members are at a hearing distance.

3. **In order to build a high-performance team, which of these is NOT done?**

   a. Have a shared team vision

   b. Set realistic goals

   c. Limit team size to 12 or less

   d. Let the team take all decisions

Solution:

d. An Agile team needs to have a shared vision that everybody believes in and agrees to the team goals. This is possible only when the team size is kept small. However, the team does not take all decisions; they take only local decisions. For example, the customer decides the priority of work items, and whether a deliverable is acceptable of not.

4. **What is the purpose of having a leader in Agile if he does not possess much power to direct the team?**

Solution:

An Agile leader performs important functions of keeping the team together, motivated, and moving towards the shared goal. Although he does not take any decisions for the team, he does facilitate the team through the decision-making process. One of the most important responsibility of the leader is to help remove impediments in the team's way. This ensures that the work progresses smoothly.

Practice Exercises

1. **Which of these is a characteristic of an empowered team?**

   a. Takes all project decisions

   b. Takes own local decisions

   c. Chooses team members on the project

   d. Prioritizes the product backlog

2. **Which of these stages represents a pseudo team?**

   a. Performing

   b. Storming

   c. Forming

   d. Norming

3. **Distributed teams can benefit MOST from?**

   a. Co-location

   b. Written documentation

   c. Tacit knowledge

   d. Use of technology in communication

*Solutions to the above questions can be downloaded from
the* **Online Resources** *section of this book on*
www.vibrantpublishers.com

This page is intentionally left blank

Glossary

Acceptance Test – testing performed for confirming the functionality expected by the user and for getting user's acceptance for one or more deliverables

Adaptive – the ability to change course rapidly

Affinity Estimating – an estimation game that has story point sizes shown in columns, and estimation is done by grouping same size user stories in the same column

Agile – an iterative and incremental approach of doing work

ATDD (Acceptance Test-Driven Development) – an agile practice from XP that promotes development of user acceptance tests in advance

Burndown Chart – a graphical tool that shows work remaining in the iteration

Burnup Chart – a graphical tool that shows work done over time (across iterations)

CFD (Cumulative Flow Diagram) – a graphical tool that shows work done and work in-progress over time (across iterations)

CPI (Cost Performance Index) – a measure that shows cost performance of the work; CPI < 1 means overspending, CPI = 1 means spending as per budget, CPI > 1 means underspending

Customer Valued Prioritization – a requirements prioritization technique that is based on value provided to the customer

Cycle Time – the amount of time it takes for a work item to complete once it is picked up for delivery

Daily Scrum Meeting – a daily collaboration meeting of the team (<= 15 minutes)

Definition of "Done" – the criteria that should be satisfied to mark a deliverable complete

EMV (Expected Monetary Value) – a quantitative technique that gives dollar value of risk exposure

Epic – a large user story

Escaped Defects – the defects found by the customer after delivery

EVM (Earned Value Management) – a schedule and cost tracking technique

Feature – a large user story

Ideal Time Estimation – a time estimation technique that assumes 100% productivity

Incremental – a delivery approach where the entire system is built piece by piece

Information Radiator – an umbrella term that includes work status related charts, graphs, and other data

Iteration – a small amount of time (1 to 4 weeks) used to build a part of the product

Iterative – a delivery approach in which a few parts of the system are built and improved upon based on customer feedback

Kanban – an agile methodology that promotes value stream management and lower work in progress

Kanban / Task Board – a graphical tool that shows work status in the iteration

Lean – a methodology closely aligned with agile and is based on waste reduction

MMP/MMF (Minimally Marketable Product / Minimally Marketable Feature) – the minimum features required in the system to make it marketable

MoSCoW – a requirements prioritization technique that separates mandatory work from optional work

MVP (Minimum Viable Product) – the features required in the system that help in getting early customer feedback

Osmotic Communication – communication that is received from the neighborhood due to close proximity

Planning Poker – an agile game used for relative sizing / estimating using poker cards (application of Wideband Delphi technique)

Potentially Shippable Product Increment – a set of deliverables completed by the end of an iteration

Product Backlog – a document containing user stories that make the product's requirements

Product Demo – a session conducted at the end of an iteration / release to showcase the deliverables to the stakeholders

Product Roadmap – a pictorial representation showing which features will be delivered in which release

Product Vision – a short statement stating the vision of the product that is to be developed

Product Owner – a role that represents the single point of contact from the business

Real Time Estimation – a time estimation technique that assumes less than 100% productivity

Refactoring – rewriting code to improve readability and maintainability without changing the functionality

Relative Sizing – a method of sizing / estimating work on a relative basis (relative to each other)

Release – a point that is achieved generally after a few iterations, when the deliverables are deployed and available for the end user to use

Release Backlog – a document containing user stories that will be taken up for delivery in the release

Release Planning Meeting – a meeting conducted at the beginning of a release to plan the work for the release

Risk-Adjusted Backlog – a product backlog that contains user stories as well risk response actions

ROI (Return On Investment) – a quantitative technique that gives dollar value of a user story

Scrum – an agile methodology that is most popular, and uses 1-4 week Sprints

ScrumMaster – a facilitator role in the Scrum methodology (servant leader)

Self-directing Team – a team that makes its own local decisions

Self-organizing Team – a team that is free from command-and-control management

Servant Leadership – the leadership style practiced in agile, where the leader serves the team and his main job is removal of impediments in the team's way

SPI (Schedule Performance Index) – a measure that shows schedule performance of the work; SPI < 1 means behind schedule, SPI = 1 means on schedule, SPI > 1 means ahead of schedule

Spike – an iteration that is taken up for the purpose of risk reduction

Sprint – an iteration in Scrum

Sprint Backlog – a document containing user stories that will be taken up for delivery in the Sprint

Sprint Planning Meeting – a meeting conducted at the beginning of a Sprint to plan the work for the Sprint

Sprint Retrospective Meeting – a meeting conducted at the end of a Sprint to discuss lessons learned in the Sprint

Sprint Review Meeting – a meeting conducted at the end of a Sprint to show completed deliverables to stakeholders

Stand-up Meeting – a daily collaboration meeting of the team (<= 15 minutes)

Story Map – a pictorial representation showing the backbone, walking skeleton, and other features, along with the release in which they would be delivered

Story Points – a unit of relative measure used for sizing / estimation of user stories

Strategy Meeting – a meeting conducted to decide high-level work planning

Tacit Knowledge – undocumented knowledge available with team members

Task – action taken to make a deliverable (same as activity)

TDD (Test-Driven Development) – an agile practice from XP that promotes development of tests in advance

Throughput – the amount of work done in a given period of time

User Story – a product requirement

Velocity – the amount (in terms of size) of work completed in an iteration

Velocity Chart – a graphical tool that shows velocity across iterations

Wideband Delphi **–** a technique to do relative sizing / estimation of user stories

WIP (Work In Progress) – work that is currently being done or partially completed work

XP (eXtreme Programming) **–** an agile methodology that is software-centric

NOTES

www.ingramcontent.com/pod-product-compliance
Lightning Source LLC
Chambersburg PA
CBHW060311220326
41598CB00027B/4296